Practical Debugging f Embedded ARM Systems

Core techniques for tracing, profiling, and fixing system-level faults

Nino Vidović

<packt>

Practical Debugging for Embedded ARM Systems

Portfolio Director: Rohit Rajkumar
Relationship Lead: Tanisha Mehrotra
Project Manager: Sandip Tadge
Content Engineer: Anuradha Joglekar
Technical Editor: Tejas Vijay Mhasvekar
Copy Editor: Safis Editing
Indexer: Tejal Soni
Proofreader: Anuradha Joglekar
Production Designer: Ajay Patule
Growth Lead: Namita Velgekar
Marketing Owner: Nivedita Pandey

First published: April 2026

Production reference: 2090626

Published by Packt Publishing Ltd.
Grosvenor House
11 St Paul's Square
Birmingham
B3 1RB, UK.

ISBN 978-1-80667-311-7
www.packtpub.com

Ich widme dieses Buch meiner Frau Franziska, sowie meinen Eltern Gordana und Samir, die mich immer unterstützt und meinen Rücken gestärkt haben.

– Nino Vidović

Foreword

The development of embedded systems is becoming increasingly complex. What once constituted a simple configuration of limited hardware resources and hand-written assembly or C code has evolved into highly sophisticated embedded platforms featuring multicore architectures, real-time operating systems, and significantly tightened requirements regarding functional safety, cybersecurity, and overall system reliability. To understand the behavior of these modern, highly complex embedded systems debugging is of crucial importance.

In *Practical Debugging for Embedded ARM Systems*, Nino Vidović shows you an insight into the world of debugging and highlights the central role it plays in modern embedded development. Debugging gives developers the visibility they need to understand the runtime behavior of their system, uncover hidden issues and make bugs visible to analyze them effectively. For embedded engineers, debugging is therefore much more than a tool. It is an indispensable component for making complex systems run stable, safely and reliably.

Nino takes you through the essential components of a typical debugging setup. He explains what is needed in practice, including hardware components such as microcontroller boards, debug probes, and debug interfaces like SWD or JTAG, as well as a suitable debugging environment or IDE. By showing how these components work together, you gain the practical understanding needed to apply the debug features and techniques presented throughout this book.

Once these fundamentals are in place, he introduces you to the basic debugging techniques that are typically built into modern embedded systems and readily accessible to developers. These include features like breakpoints, printf debugging, debug state control, usage of call stack and disassembly for debugging. Basic debugging techniques are often sufficient for finding simple issues, but they can disturb system timing and hide real problems. To go beyond these limitations, Nino provides insight into advanced debugging methods that allow deeper, non-intrusive analysis of embedded systems. He explains advanced debugging features like software and hardware tracing,

variable and power profiling, RTOS awareness, and monitor mode debugging.

How this toolbox of debugging techniques can be combined to quickly solve problems is demonstrated in real-world examples such as crash analysis, watchdog handling, and several others.

A key strength of this book is its strong practical focus. Both the basic and advanced techniques, as well as the real-world examples, are illustrated through images, linked videos, and code examples. This supporting material makes the concepts easier to understand and apply in practice, offering clear guidance for beginners while still providing meaningful insights for more experienced embedded developers.

I wish you an enjoyable read, and I hope this book helps you to solve real-world problems more effectively with the help of debugging.

Patrick Kirner-Fehrenbach

Embedded Software Engineer, fellow student, and friend

Contributors

About the author

Nino Vidović is a senior software engineer and product owner at SEGGER Microcontroller GmbH, specializing in embedded systems and real-time application debugging. He manages the J-Trace product line, crucial for enhancing developers' efficiency and accuracy. Nino earned his Bachelor's and Master's degrees in Microsystems Engineering from the IMTEK Institute at the University of Freiburg and conducted advanced research in MEMS engineering at the Fraunhofer IMS. He also spearheads the SEGGER Educational Partnership Program, bridging academia and industry. Nino's technical expertise is complemented by his dedication to education, driving innovation while empowering the next generation of engineers.

I would like to extend my thanks to my wife and my kids for being very understanding that I needed to put in many evening hours to make this book come true.

I would like to thank Amar Mahmutbegović for connecting me with the Packt team and big thanks to Tanisha Mehrotra for keeping track of everything and making this book possible.

Special thanks go out to Anuradha Vishwas Joglekar, Alexander Uwah, and Christoph Sax for their valuable input and time in reviewing this book and to the entire Packt team for their support during the course of writing this book.

About the reviewers

Christoph Sax is an embedded systems engineer working on advances debug and trace solutions for embedded platforms. Since joining Lauterbach over a decade ago, he has gained experience across multiple areas of the debug tool ecosystem. Currently, he focuses on applying debug and trace technology to safety-critical projects, providing customers with guidance on all aspects of trace-based code coverage and tool qualification.

He lives with his lovely wife in Munich, Germany. They enjoy music, traveling, and Asian cuisine.

Alexander Uwah has a strong foundation in the semiconductor industry where he has spent most of his time at major global companies like Intel, Infineon and Microchip. The wealth of his 25+ years career ranges from expertise in deeply embedded firmware running on millions of smartphones, over system-level verification based on virtual prototyping as well as emulation technologies and extends to development of desktop and server-based software solutions of various kinds in corporate environments. He has furthermore filled various roles of managing and leading teams in different areas of product development. Besides technology, he loves creating music on tangible instruments, admiring nature and spending time with his wife and 2 daughters.

Table of Contents

Chapter 3: Basic Debugging Features   27

Preface

Have you ever wondered how embedded debugging works, or if you are making most of the setup that is already available to you?

Well, then you picked up the right book as these are the questions I will try to answer.

My main motivation to write this book was realizing that there is an astonishing knowledge gap within the embedded community when it comes to debugging. Be it students just getting into the domain or even well-versed software engineers that already work and produce code in that domain for a couple of years.

A big portion of embedded software engineers have not learned about the different debug techniques and features that are available to them. In most university curriculum it is merely a sidenote and in the best-case scenario one might learn about `printf`-debugging. So, all knowledge that is available is typically learned on the job.

To fill that gap, I created this book with the goal of providing information that, in my opinion, is not available in a condensed form out there.

The other more self-preserving motivation is a direct implication of sharing this knowledge. Chances are that I will be using products at some point developed by you or other readers and the better you are equipped to debug code faults, the better and safer the products should be. Or at least I hope so.

At the end of the book, you should be equipped with a broad arsenal of various debug features and methods which you can apply to real-world scenarios. While the books' focus is on the Arm chip architecture and its debug features, the concepts and features that are introduced in this book are usually universally applicable to the embedded domain.

The book will offer various visualizations, videos, and example code to be able to follow along through the different debugging techniques and features.

It is, however, not meant as "yet another how-to guide", so be aware that some basic background knowledge may be required.

Who this book is for

This book is for intermediate embedded developers who already know how to build and flash ARM-based firmware but want to level up their debugging skills. It is ideal for firmware engineers, embedded software developers, and engineers transitioning from basic development to professional, tool-driven debugging workflows.

What this book covers

Chapter 1, A Brief History of Embedded Systems Debugging, covers the history embedded systems debugging. From the early beginnings to modern debug tools and trends.

Chapter 2, What Is Debugging and Why Should You Care?, defines what debugging generally is and how it can be integrated into embedded development workflows. The chapter will cover basic setup components, their typical price ranges, and the various debug interface standards.

Chapter 3, Basic Debugging Features, introduces the basic debug concepts and features which are available on most modern embedded devices. This chapter will show concepts on how to tackle certain issues with each feature and how it can be used to the developer's advantage.

Chapter 4, Advanced Debugging Features, expands the previous chapter and introduces more advanced debug concepts. While some of these features may not always be available or are more expensive to use, they can give a valuable deeper insight in your running system.

Chapter 5, From Theory to Practice, focuses on common real-world issues and shows the reader how the learned debug features and techniques can be applied most effectively to quickly remove these common bugs.

To get the most out of this book

Ideally you already have basic knowledge about Arm microcontrollers and how they generally work.

In *Chapters 4* and *5*, there will be example projects, which you can follow along if you want to. However, it is completely optional as all scenarios and features introduced in this book will be accompanied by screenshots, detailed explanations, and sometimes even videos, so it is not required to try to follow the examples with your own setup.

But to include all learning types, here is the hardware and software requirements if you plan on replicating the scenarios from the book:

- J-Trace Pro Cortex-M V3
- Renesas EK-RA8M1 Board Version 1 with on-board debug probe
- Cortex-M Trace Reference Board V1.2 (based on ST STM32F407)
- SEGGER Embedded Studio IDE V8.26
- Ozone debug software V3.40c
- SystemView V3.62c

Download the example code files

The code bundle for the book is hosted on GitHub at `https://github.com/PacktPublishing/-Practical-Debugging-for-Embedded-ARM-Systems`. We also have other code bundles from our rich catalog of books and videos available at `https://github.com/PacktPublishing`. Check them out!

Download the color images

We also provide a PDF file that has color images of the screenshots/diagrams used in this book. You can download it here:`https://packt.link/gbp/9781806673117`.

Check out the video material

To check out the live demonstration of examples, go to`https://packt.link/jDMTz`, or scan the following QR code:

Conventions used

There are a number of text conventions used throughout this book.

`CodeInText`: Indicates code words in text, database table names, folder names, filenames, file extensions, pathnames, dummy URLs, user input, and Twitter handles. For example: "We comment out `_DivideByZero()` and comment in `_IllegalWrite()`."

A block of code is set as follows:

```
Break.SetOnSrc ("main.c:61");
Break.SetOnSrc ("SEGGER_THUMB_Startup.s:199");
//
//   Set Function which should be executed once BP is hit
//
Break.SetCommand("main.c:61","OnBPHitMain");
Break.SetCommand("SEGGER_THUMB_Startup.s:199","OnBPHitExit");
```

When we wish to draw your attention to a particular part of a code block, the relevant lines or items are set in bold:

```
Break.SetOnSrc ("main.c:61");
Break.SetOnSrc ("SEGGER_THUMB_Startup.s:199");
//
// Set Function which should be executed once BP is hit
//
Break.SetCommand("main.c:61","OnBPHitMain");
Break.SetCommand("SEGGER_THUMB_Startup.s:199","OnBPHitExit");
```

Any command-line input or output is written as follows:

```
terraform init
```

Bold: Indicates a new term, an important word, or words that you see on the screen. For instance, words in menus or dialog boxes appear in the text like this. For example: "You can do that in Ozone via **Tools| Trace Settings | Trace Source | Trace Pins**."

> **Note**
>
> Warnings or important notes appear like this.

> **Tip**
>
> Tips and tricks appear like this.

Get in touch

Feedback from our readers is always welcome.

General feedback: If you have questions about any aspect of this book or have any general feedback, please email us at customercare@packt.com and mention the book's title in the subject of your message.

Errata: Although we have taken every care to ensure the accuracy of our content, mistakes do happen. If you have found a mistake in this book, we would be grateful if you reported this to us. Please visit http://www.packt.com/submit-errata, click **Submit Errata**, and fill in the form.

Piracy: If you come across any illegal copies of our works in any form on the internet, we would be grateful if you would provide us with the location address or website name. Please contact us at copyright@packt.com with a link to the material.

If you are interested in becoming an author: If there is a topic that you have expertise in and you are interested in either writing or contributing to a book, please visit http://authors.packt.com/.

Free benefits with your book

This book comes with free benefits to support your learning. Activate them now for instant access (see the "*How to Unlock*" section for instructions).

Here's a quick overview of what you can instantly unlock with your purchase:

DRM-Free PDF Version

Download DRM-free PDF and ePub copies of this book.

7-Day Packt Library Access

Get 7-day unlimited access to 8,000+ books and videos. No credit card required.

Available for first-time Packt+ trial users only.

Next-Gen Reader Access

Read this book on Packt Reader with progress sync, dark mode and note-taking.

How to Unlock

Scan the QR code (or go to `packtpub.com/unlock`). Search for this book by name, confirm the edition, and then follow the steps on the page.

Note: Keep your invoice handy. Purchases made directly from Packt don't require one

Share your thoughts

Once you've read *Practical Debugging for Embedded ARM Systems*, we'd love to hear your thoughts! Scan the QR code below to go straight to the Amazon review page for this book and share your feedback.

https://packt.link/r/1806673118

Your review is important to us and the tech community and will help us make sure we're delivering excellent quality content.

1

A Brief History of Embedded Systems Debugging

Embedded systems debugging is an extensive topic that is crucial to the modern embedded domain. In this book, I want to teach you why debugging is crucial, which fundamentals are important, and introduce more advanced debug topics such as instruction tracing and power profiling. You will learn about various debug features and techniques, and by the end of the book, you should be capable of applying the newly acquired knowledge to tackle real-world problems.

The book will give concise, sufficient information to provide a solid understanding of each topic, and include references and keywords for further, deeper study if desired.

Before getting into the technical details of embedded systems debugging, I want to start off with a little bit of historical background, so we can better understand how we got to the technologies that we have today, and maybe also gain some appreciation for the people who came before us and have paved the path for what we are using today.

In this chapter, we'll cover the following topics:

- Early beginnings of embedded systems
- The birth of debugging tools
- Evolution of programming languages
- The rise of Integrated Development Environments (IDEs)
- Modern challenges and trends

Early beginnings of embedded systems

In the beginning, there was chaos and uncertainty. Systems were running raw byte code, and debug interfaces were scarce or even nonexistent.

Arguably, one of the first embedded systems was the **Apollo Guidance Computer** (**AGC**), which was released in 1966 and was used for multiple Apollo missions [1].

It featured a tightly integrated system with very capable hardware specifications for its time.

- 1 MHz CPU clock speed
- ~69 kB of ROM
- ~3,8 kB of RAM
- 32 kg total system weight

By today's metrics, the clock speed may appear very low, but surprisingly, the typical memory sizes of modern microcontrollers are sometimes still of a similar magnitude as the APC's memory was.

But we all know about the famous success of the Apollo missions, so while these resources appear microscopic these days, they were plentiful for their intended purpose.

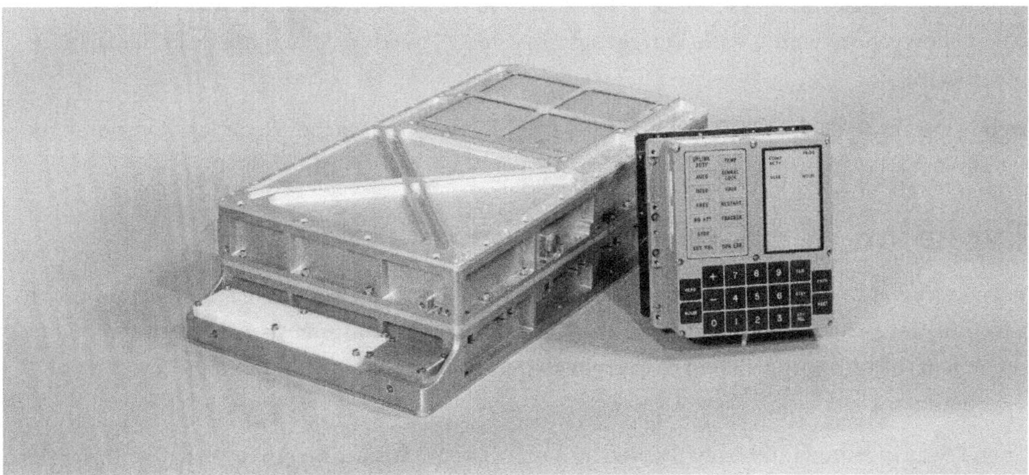

Figure 1.1: Front view of the AGC

However, debugging the software that was running on the system was tedious due to the lack of proper debug features that were integrated into the chip's architecture. Typically, debugging was done indirectly via light indicators or simple `print` statements to a terminal.

Luckily, analyzing the assembly source code manually was relatively straightforward as the complete available memory was just 2,048 words. Even though the application featured a rudimentary RTOS and multiple algorithms for different calculation tasks, it could be analyzed quickly.

The birth of debugging tools

Over time, in the 1970s, **system-specific software debuggers (monitor debuggers)** started appearing that allowed inspecting memory locations, using breakpoints, and controlling the execution flow of the program.

However, these debuggers resided in the system's memory, and on resource-constrained systems, it was not ideal.

Next, in the 1980s and 1990s, we saw the birth of **in-circuit emulators (ICEs)**. These huge boxes allowed interacting with a target system directly, making debugging tasks in real-time possible [2].

Debug interfaces such as JTAG additionally standardized approaches to debug environments for embedded systems, bringing costs down [3].

Evolution of programming languages

Initially, there was just machine code for computers. To make them more readable for humans, **assembly language** was introduced in the 1960s. It was predominantly used in the embedded domain in the beginning, due to the very resource-constrained systems and precise control over hardware.

Then **C** was invented in 1972. It allowed structural programming on embedded systems with a balance between high-level software abstraction and low-level hardware access. Until this day, C is still the most used programming language for embedded systems [4].

During the 1980s, the first **object-oriented programming** language, **ADA**, was introduced with the main goal of code safety and maintainability. That is why it was mostly utilized in avionics [5].

In 1985, **C++** was released, another object-oriented approach, which initially did not have embedded real-time systems specifically in mind but gained much popularity over the years due to its flexibility and great language support [6].

In the 1990s, **Java** was introduced to the software world, promising excellent cross-compatibility over all available platforms. It took over the world of general computing quickly, and for embedded systems, it paved the way for modern smartphones and IoT devices [7].

At the same time, scripting languages such as Python started to gain more popularity. These days, Python is one of the most popular programming languages and can even be cross-compiled to embedded systems as well [8].

With its very simple and easy to learn syntax, Python has taken over many software engineering disciplines in a flash.

In the 2010s, **Rust** was introduced, and while it took some time to be established in the embedded domain, its innovative ownership model for memory management promised memory-safe applications, eliminating some of the most common bug types in the software development domain [9].

The rise of Integrated Development Environments (IDEs)

Most debugging was initially done via terminal prints and command-line interfaces.

Build systems were usually separate systems, making testing code iterations cumbersome.

To improve this situation in the 1980s, so-called **Integrated Development Environments (IDEs)** were introduced, making code writing, building, and debugging all happen inside the same, usually GUI-based tool.

This not only streamlined development setups but also gave tremendous advantages in the time-to-market race.

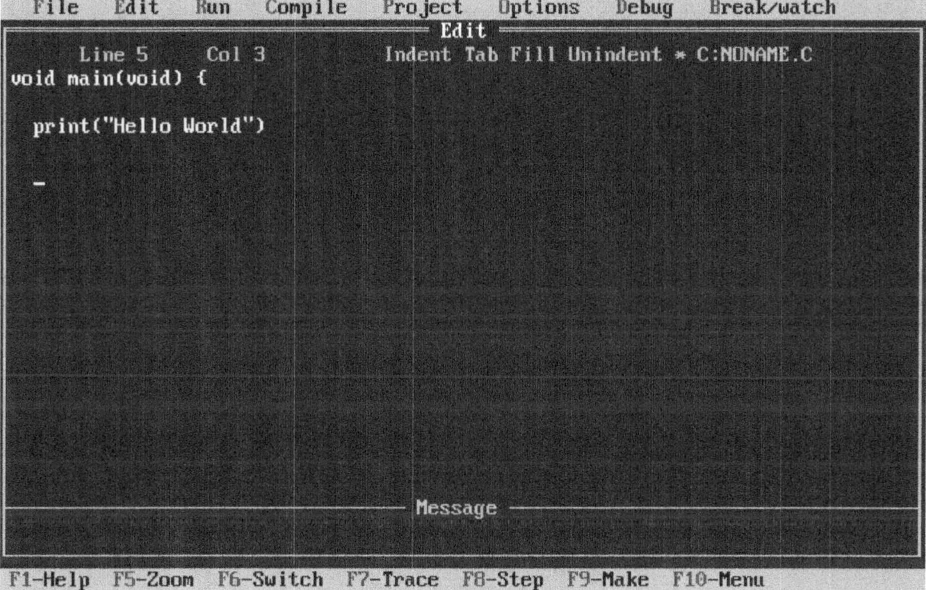

Figure 1.2: Turbo C IDE

Here, we can see one of the first C IDEs, called **Turbo C,** which was available for DOS systems. It featured a text editor, project management features, a debugger, a build environment, and much more.

However, specifically at the beginning, using IDEs was frowned upon as experienced users argued that IDEs would limit their creative freedom [10].

But as history shows us, IDEs came to stay and are available these days on many systems in many flavors, for all kinds of programming languages.

Modern challenges and trends

So far, we have learned about the past of embedded systems debugging. We came from rather rudimentary debug features and environments to rather sophisticated setups with plentiful features.

But what does a modern landscape in the 2020s look like, and what are the current challenges and trends?

One great development is that nearly all modern microcontrollers that are released these days have debug ports integrated, even with some advanced debug features that go along with it. This led to a great availability of all kinds of debug probes that offer solutions for a broad range of budgets and chip architectures.

There are even on-board variants available, so whole debug probes can be tightly integrated into your own board designs.

The broad availability of debug interfaces and probes with advanced debug features makes bug hunting as efficient as it has ever been before.

Features such as hardware and software tracing, live memory manipulation, various breakpoint types, and many more will be covered in this book in more detail, so you can make the most of these modern features that are available even on the cheapest microcontrollers these days.

However, we also see that target systems are becoming increasingly complex. Multi-core devices are becoming the norm, complex memory management schemes become necessary, and advanced safety features increase the learning curve for newcomers to the embedded domain. So, having advanced debug setups becomes a necessity at some point.

To counter the trend of more complex devices, we see an increasing trend of third-party hardware abstraction layers and code generators being used to reduce the initial complexity of a new system. The trade-off is, however, that third-party code blobs are added to your software, where the chain of trust may become watered down, which, in the worst case, may add unwanted security risks to your application.

We also see the rise of embedded frameworks such as Zephyr that take the abstractions even further. Whether eliminating hardware dependencies will be the cure for future complex embedded systems, only time will tell, but it is definitely an approach that you should use consciously, as program safety is also becoming a core factor of modern embedded systems.

Another popular trend is the rapid rise to fame of Visual Studio Code from Microsoft. Starting off as a feature-rich free text editor with a plugin interface and built-in community features, it quickly transformed into a one-size-fits-all platform for modern software development, even in the embedded domain, challenging market-leading IDEs.

A more classic approach to counter complexity that is gaining much ground in the embedded domain is automated unit testing on embedded systems. Typically, such tests are run in separate simulation environments, oftentimes in the form of digital twins. However, many have now painfully learned that nothing beats testing on the actual hardware. Due to short prototyping cycles, quick availability of PCBs is becoming the norm, thus allowing testing on hardware early in a development cycle.

Last but not least, there's **artificial intelligence (AI)** in the form of **large language models (LLMs)**. It is here now, so we have to talk about the elephant in the room. It can already write mostly correct code. It can somewhat debug broken code, but what it excels at is being a valuable assistant to an experienced developer. Even in the embedded domain where the training data for AI models is quite scarce and not always easily machine-readable, many of the suggestions and help you can receive from AI can still boost your productivity, and most importantly, it saves precious time when digging through thousands of pages of documentation, because what LLMs do best is pattern recognition of language context.

But what current LLMs also do very well is hallucinate answers, since current AI companies tune their models to give the user answers that would make them happy to keep engagement with the platform high, instead of always providing accurate information.

That is, of course, not ideal if you are trying to get a correct answer in a mostly deterministic profession such as software engineering. But LLM companies promise that this will all be fixed soon, and we just have to wait a bit longer.

History seems to be on their side, as so far, anything that humans could think or dream of in the technical domain was at some point later realized, so the chances are good that this will also happen with AI. But whether it will happen during my lifetime, I do not know. I am still waiting for cold fusion and teleportation.

But let's focus on reality and on what we humans do best – teaching each other new things, which, hopefully, will be achieved by the end of this book.

Summary

In this chapter, we learned about the history of embedded systems debugging, from the early beginnings, the first actual embedded systems, to modern interfaces, programming languages, and debugging tools.

Next, let's try to find out exactly what debugging is, why it is important, which peculiarities appear in the embedded domain, and what kind of debug interfaces exist.

References

1. The Virtual AGC Project Spaceborne Computer Systems: `https://www.ibiblio.org/apollo/#gsc.tab=0`

2. Debugging stories: from printf, just Flash and beyond, Erol Simsek, 2022: `https://www.embedded.com/debugging-stories-from-printf-just-flash-and-beyond`

3. IEEE Standard for Test Access Port and Boundary-Scan Architecture, IEEE Std. 1149.1-2013, 2013. IEEE.

4. Ritchie, D. M., & Kernighan, B. W. (1988). The C programming language (2nd ed.). Prentice Hall.

5. Burns, A., & Wellings, A. J. (2007). Concurrent and Real-Time Programming in Ada. Cambridge University Press.

6. Stroustrup, B. (2013). The C++ programming language (4th ed.). Addison-Wesley.

7. Gosling, J., Holmes, B., & Steel, G. (1996). The Java Language Specification. Addison-Wesley.

8. Lutz, M. (1996). Programming Python (1st ed.). O'Reilly Media.

9. Klabnik, S., & Nichols, K. (2018). The Rust Programming Language. No Starch Press.

10. Raymond, E. (2003). The Art of Unix Programming

Get this book's PDF version and more

Scan the QR code (or go to `packtpub.com/unlock`). Search for this book by name, confirm the edition, and then follow the steps on the page.

Note: Keep your invoice handy. Purchases made directly from Packt don't require an invoice.

2

What Is Debugging and Why Should You Care?

First, we need to understand what debugging is, why it is important for modern embedded systems development, and how it can be applied to your particular existing workflow.

In this chapter, you will understand the significance of debugging. We will start with a typical debug setup and then go into the details of the essential components. You will gain insights into the cost brackets associated with different debugging scenarios, helping you understand budget considerations.

Additionally, common debug interfaces will be discussed, explaining their functionalities. Finally, you will learn how debugging integrates into your existing development workflow, emphasizing its importance in ensuring efficient programming and problem-solving.

In this chapter, we'll cover the following topics:

- What is debugging?
- Bare-metal environments and operating systems
- Debug interfaces and environments
- Typical cost brackets for debug setups
- How does a debug setup fit in your development workflow?

Technical requirements

This specific chapter does not have any technical requirements as it does not contain any
example code.

What is debugging?

Let's begin with the definition of the word **debugging**. If we look it up on Wikipedia, we will
find the following definition [1]:

> *In engineering, debugging is the process of finding the root cause, workarounds, and possible fixes for*
> *bugs.*

In other words, debugging is the process of analyzing so-called bugs and ideally removing
them. Bugs are program defects or unwanted behaviors that need to be resolved.

Historically, the term *bug* was used as early as the 19th century by Thomas Edison to describe
defects in his inventions. However, the term *debugging* was coined much later by Admiral Grace
Hopper in the 1940s, who was working on one of the early models of electromechanical
computers at Harvard. Her team discovered a moth trapped in the relays causing malfunctions
on the computer. They removed the moth (that is, the bug) and jokingly noted that the
computer was now debugged [2].

Okay, now we know what debugging in general is. But what about embedded debugging? Well,
now it becomes a bit more complicated as we need to define what an embedded system even is.

Let's reference Wikipedia once more [3]:

> *An embedded system is a specialized computer system—a combination of a computer processor,*
> *computer memory, and input/output peripheral devices—that has a dedicated function within a*
> *larger mechanical or electronic system. It is embedded as part of a complete device often including*
> *electrical or electronic hardware and mechanical parts. Because an embedded system typically controls*
> *physical operations of the machine that it is embedded within, it often has real-time computing*
> *constraints.*

Wikipedia defines an embedded system as a computer that is part of a larger system. This
broad description is of what I personally would call "small embedded" systems. This includes
all systems and setups that are usually microcontroller-based, tightly integrated into (usually)
small circuit boards, and mostly running bare-metal code with direct hardware control.

What the Wikipedia definition does not cover immediately is what I would call "large embedded" systems. They are mainly based on more powerful microprocessors that usually boot up a full **operating system (OS)**, which is typically something such as an embedded Linux system.

This gives the developer access to a full-fledged OS that is usually known from desktop PCs and the like, with all their advantages and disadvantages. What they are will be revealed in the next section.

Bare-metal environments and OSs

On embedded systems, we have to distinguish between three main software architecture types [4][5]:

- **Bare-metal**
- **Real-Time Operating System (RTOS)**
- **General-Purpose Operating System (GPOS)**

Let's first look into GPOS environments. The OS manages hardware resources, provides services, and manages user rights. When developing software for such a system, the GPOS will take care of all required resources, such as memory management, as well as loading libraries and handling other dependencies. The application usually interacts with the system over high-level abstraction layers and **Application Programming Interfaces (APIs)**. Debugging tools are usually readily available and tightly integrated in the OS and surrounding software stack.

A typical OS layer stack looks as follows [6]:

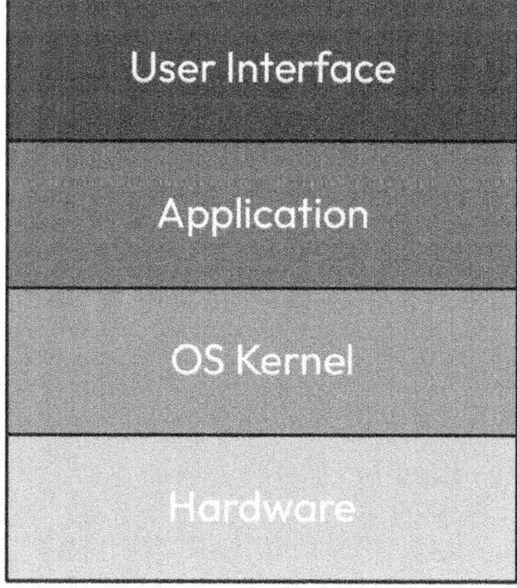

Figure 2.1: Typical OS layer stack

Let's take a look at each layer in detail:

- **User interface**: This handles interactions with the OS user. Both graphical and command-line interfaces are possible.

- **Application**: This is the application that is running on top of the OS, usually started by the user to fulfill some task. There are also background processes that might have been started by the OS. In any case, they are applications that run within their own assigned memory space dictated by the OS. Trying to break out of that space allocated by the OS will lead to an application crash.

- **OS kernel**: This provides core functions for the OS itself and the layers above it, such as process scheduling, memory management, device management, filesystem, user permission management, and a system call API layer between kernel and user space.

- **Hardware**: This layer contains all hardware abstraction layers, device drivers, network drivers, and so on that are necessary for the kernel layer to be able to directly access the available hardware and communication interfaces so the layers above can fulfill their tasks.

All of this makes such environments excellent setups for general-purpose applications, which should run on as many systems as possible.

The biggest drawback of such GPOS environments is that they are usually not real-time-capable and thus are not usable for many applications and industries typically rooted in the functional safety domain, where software that can't meet specific timing constraints might cause serious real-world damage.

Additionally, GPOS environments are highly complex setups with many different software stacks interacting with each other that are usually not maintained or supported by one entity. This can make issues hard to track down as each contributor to the software stack relies on the correctness of other software components.

While we typically know such setups from desktop computers and notebooks, they are also available in the embedded domain. The most prominent of these systems that most of us interact with every day is a smartphone.

But this book will not focus on such GPOS environments. Instead, we will look at bare-metal and RTOS setups. So, what is the difference?

The biggest difference is that on a bare-metal embedded system, the developer is usually directly accessing the hardware layer, which gives them maximum control over the environment. The main goal is to extract as much usable code and performance out of resource-constrained chips as possible.

This brings us to the biggest advantages of bare-metal setups: execution speed and reactivity to events. With a bare-metal setup, you can ensure specific timing constraints that would simply be impossible with a GPOS.

However, there are some trade-offs, including limited portability to different hardware platforms and no managed user space with easy-to-use application layers for easy-to-write general-purpose applications.

Everything you do in bare metal may need to be done from scratch for your particular hardware platform.

By adding an RTOS layer, we regain some of the benefits from a GPOS while keeping the direct hardware access benefits.

A quick summary of the benefits and drawbacks of the different embedded software architecture types can be found in this table:

Types	Advantages	Disadvantages
Bare metal	High performance	Complex development
Bare metal	High efficiency	Limited portability
Bare metal	Direct hardware control	Limited scalability
RTOS	Deterministic timing	Increased overhead
RTOS	Multitasking	Higher resource footprint
RTOS	Better portability	More complex debugging
GPOS	Easier maintenance	Performance overhead
GPOS	Highly scalable	No real-time performance
GPOS	Quick time to market	Many binary blobs

Table 2.1: Comparison between different embedded software architecture types

However, it is not always as black and white as we've discussed. In truth, many modern "small" embedded systems are not necessarily fully bare metal. They rely on third-party drivers or hardware abstraction layers or use RTOSs. While such an approach might sacrifice some of the benefits from a completely bare-metal system, it gains benefits from the GPOS setup when it comes to portability, time to market, and easier software scalability.

But what is usually kept is direct control over your hardware and peripherals.

So far, we have learned about the different embedded software architecture types. But what about debugging such setups? Let's see.

Debug environments

One big advantage of GPOS environments is that on most systems, basic debug components are either already included or very easily accessible. As all applications run in their own defined user space on top of the OS, we can simply hook into the running process and debug it. All essential information for the debug tool is provided through the OS and its API layers so that we can get maximum insight into our application that is meant to be debugged.

Here's the typical debug workflow on GPOS environments:

1. Build the application.

2. Launch the application through a debugger or stand-alone, and then attach the debugger to the running process.

3. Take control over your application with the debugger and start analyzing and debugging it.

On bare-metal embedded systems, the setup is a bit different. As we already established, we do not have a GPOS running with all tools, libraries, and so on pre-installed that provide the debugger with all of the necessary information to analyze the application. Instead, nothing is set up yet, as the application that we are building is not even loaded on the microcontroller yet. So, here's how the debug workflow on bare-metal environments can look like:

1. The first step starts on a host PC. Here, we build our application for our processor architectures in the target chip. The resulting file is typically some form of a binary file that now must be programmed to the target device's nonvolatile memory, called **Flash**. This is typically done via some hardware interface between the developer PC and the target device. The most common interfaces are UART and JTAG.

2. Wire up the host PC with the target device. We need some kind of device that is usually connected via USB to the host PC and via the debug interface on the target device side. The resulting debug setup for an embedded device can look as follows:

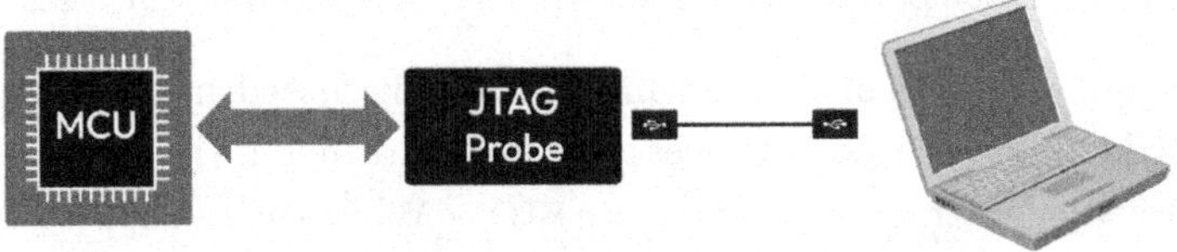

Figure 2.2: Example embedded debug setup

3. Once the connection is set up, we can program the target device. Depending on the hardware interface to the target device and the capabilities of the debug probe, we can now also control the target device's execution and system state and thus debug it in the way that we are familiar with from a GPOS environment.

On the developer PC side, there will be some sort of software debugger that will communicate with the debug probe and thus be able to interact with the target device.

There are many different variants of debug probes. The most common are on-board variants that are tightly integrated with the target hardware board itself and external probes, as pictured in *Figure 2.2*, which give more flexibility and portability.

In any case, these probes need to communicate with something on the chip to receive the required information to provide the developer PC debug software with all of the necessary information about the target device system state to be able to debug it.

The module that is being communicated with is usually an on-chip debug port with varying feature sets. The communication protocol is usually based on some industrial standard, which will be addressed in more detail in the following sections.

The following list summarizes the minimum requirements for an embedded debug setup:

- Host PC with debug software and build target application
- Debug probe (external or on-board)
- Debug interface connector on target board
- Target device with debug port

These days, most modern microcontrollers fulfill the minimum requirements and thus can usually be debugged with a debug probe. This was not always the case with older—for example, 8-bit—microcontrollers.

The main platform that will be referenced in the examples in later chapters is based on an Arm Cortex-M85 and Cortex-M4 target device.

Now that we have learned what a bare-metal environment is and what components are required to establish a connection between the developer PC and the target device, let's understand how much such a setup costs.

Typical cost brackets for debug setups

In the following cost brackets, the cost for the host PC or laptop is not included. So, keep in mind that you will need some form of host system that you write and debug your target application from.

The cost brackets for hardware debug setups can be roughly split into the following tiers:

	Tier 1	Tier 2	Tier 3	Tier 4
Description	Private/educational	Basic commercial	Advanced commercial	Specialized commercial
Price Range	5–100€	100–500€	500–10,000€	>10,000€
Ideal for	Students, hobbyists	Every embedded engineer	Every embedded engineering team	Niche setups with a small user base
Example image				

Table 2.2: Cost brackets for hardware debug setups

As you can see from *Table 2.2*, there is a debug setup available for each budget range.

Technically, you can even get it for "free" if you purchase an evaluation board platform that comes with an on-board debugger. However, there is still some cost involved; it is just hidden in the board's retail price. As honorable mention, there is technically a completely free debug setup possible if you are using a hardware simulator like QEMU. But that would be a topic for another book.

For now, let's focus on the information in the table and discuss each tier in detail:

- **Tier 1**: With tier 1, you can already get quite capable debug setups. Typically, these are either open source probes, on-board probes on evaluation boards, or silicon vendor-specific probes. Their goal is to get you started cheaply. Drawbacks are usually limited support, feature sets, and performance.
- This is a perfect fit for beginners, students, or very cost-aware customers.

- **Tier 2**: With tier 2, you get into the commercial probe domain. Here, performance, support, and versatility are the key selling points. Typically, the user experience is taken into account so you can get started quickly. There is support for a higher degree of automation, which can save a lot of time for users. If you run into issues, you usually have access to a technical support team that will assist you swiftly, so you do not waste precious time on setup issues. There are also plenty of probe vendors that are independent, so you do not have the risk of vendor lock-in. This tier is the perfect fit for any professional embedded developer who needs reliable tools to get their work done efficiently.

- **Tier 3**: Tier 3 unlocks further advanced debug features, such as instruction tracing, data sampling, and power profiling. While you will most likely not need such features daily, it is good to have probes with such capabilities available in your toolbox for scenarios where basic debug features are simply not sufficient anymore.

- **Tier 4**: Tier 4 is for niche custom cores or emulation setups where there is no or just a limited tooling ecosystem around it. Essentially, you have to build your own tools, which obviously comes at a higher cost. These are typically not widespread setups and are usually used only in very specific industrial contexts.

> **Note**
>
> Prices may, of course, change over time, and future technologies might require an expansion of the tier list in *Table 2.2*, but it shows the current state of the market and how the typical budgets are partitioned.

The key takeaway from this table is that there is an embedded debug setup available for every budget, so money should never be an argument for skipping a debug setup. Why: we will learn in *Chapters 3* to *5*.

Debug interfaces

Debug interfaces are the key element connecting your debug probe to the target device's debug port.

Ideally, you have a hardware designer in your team who handles all aspects of the debug interface, including connections, but it is never a bad idea to know the fundamentals yourself.

In this section, we will go over the main debug interfaces that are available on Arm Cortex-M target devices. You will learn about the different pinouts, the available connectors, and their specific advantages and disadvantages [7].

JTAG

We will kick things off with the absolute classic, **JTAG**. This interface is named after the **Joint Test Action Group**, which ratified the standard.

The original standard was ratified in 1990, and its initial purpose was the automated testing of printed circuit boards. The interface could be used to test the interconnectivity of all pins of a chip package and external components without needing access to every pin.

That feature is called a **boundary scan**. With more modern microcontrollers, the JTAG interface was expanded and can now be used to directly interface with the Arm **Debug Access Port (DAP)**.

Via DAP, you get access to the core, different memory regions (Flash and RAM), and the peripheral registers. That way, you can control the state and memory of the microcontroller, and thus the interface can be used for debugging and programming [7].

For a debug probe to be able to connect via JTAG, it must be connected to the specified JTAG pins and support the JTAG protocol.

The JTAG signals are as follows:

- **Test Data In (TDI)**
- **Test Data Out (TDO)**
- **Test Clock (TCK)**
- **Test Mode Select (TMS)**
- **Test Reset (TRST)**

One of the standout features of JTAG is the option to daisy chain multiple devices via the same JTAG connector. To do this, the TCK and TMS of all devices are interconnected. Then, the TDI of the first device in the chain is connected to the debug probe. The TDO of the first device is connected to the TDI pin of the next device in the chain. This is repeated until the last device in the chain is reached. The TDO of the last device is connected to the debug probe. The JTAG daisy chain is then ready to be utilized. In the case of the TRST, it depends on the used target devices and what to do with them. You can either interconnect them all to be controlled by the debug probe or pull them high to keep the devices out of reset. In some cases, the TRST connection is even optional. This is typically done on the PCB design side, so you still use the same connector as if it were a single device.

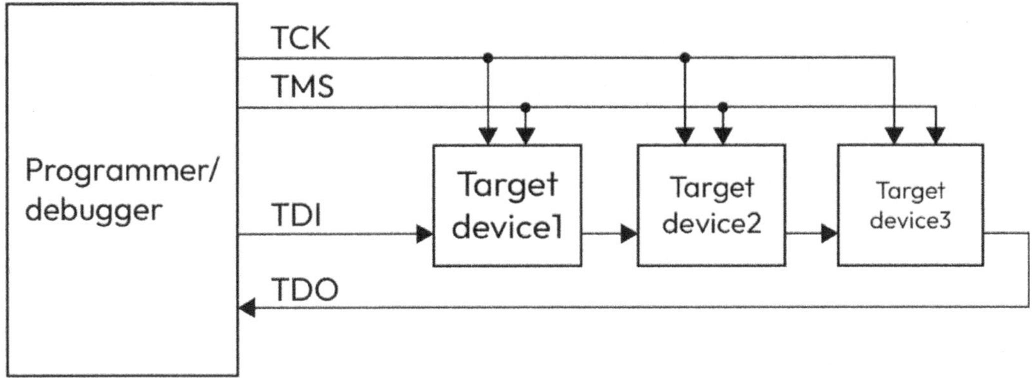

Figure 2.3: Sketch of a JTAG daisy chain setup

Not only are the pins themselves and the protocol standardized, but also the connector between the debug probe and the JTAG connector. In the case of Arm Cortex-M, there are several connector standards referenced by Arm. In the *Pinouts and additional pins* section, we will go over the different connectors in more detail.

As a side note, there is also a low-pin-count JTAG variant available for microcontrollers called **compact JTAG (cJTAG)**, specified in IEEE 1149.7. However, it is not very widespread in the Arm ecosystem as Arm has its own low-pin-count debug interface, but it is becoming more popular with RISC-V-based microcontrollers.

SWD

The **Serial Wire Debug (SWD)** port is specified by Arm and was created with the goal of reducing the pin count for the debug interface [7].

The reasoning is simply that JTAG requires at least four pins (if we ignore TRST and set it to permanently high via a pull-up resistor). Four pins are, in many instances, simply too many, especially in low-count chip housings that are still widespread, such as 16- to 32-pin. In such form factors, every pin counts.

So, Arm's solution is SWD. Instead of four pins, only two are required. The SWD signals are the following:

- **Serial Wire Debug Input/Output (SWDIO)**
- **Serial Wire Clock (SWCLK)**

There is an optional third pin called **Serial Wire Output (SWO)**, which can be used for additional debug features.

Via SWD, you get access to the same debug port as if you were using JTAG. Most target devices even support both debug interfaces.

> **Note**
>
> **Multi-drop support**
>
> As honorable mention, SWD also supports the so-called **multi-drop**, which allows to connect multiple target devices in parallel via the same two pins. However, unlike JTAG, it is just an optional feature, and it is implementation-defined if you can chain together multiple chips from the same silicon vendor or not. So, make sure to check your target device's reference manual if SWD multi-drop is supported and if the debug probe you are using also has multi-drop support.

Next, let's take a look at the respective connector pinouts of the JTAG and SWD interfaces.

Pinout and additional pins

Now it is time to learn about the purpose of the standard debug interface pins and all extra pins that are not covered by the default SWD or JTAG pins.

Let's begin with the legacy ARM JTAG and SWD connectors. They both use a 0.1-inch pitch, have 20 pins, and are keyed, so plugging them in the wrong orientation is theoretically impossible.

The official name in the Arm documentation is simply **ARM standard JTAG connector** [8].

The pinout diagram is as follows:

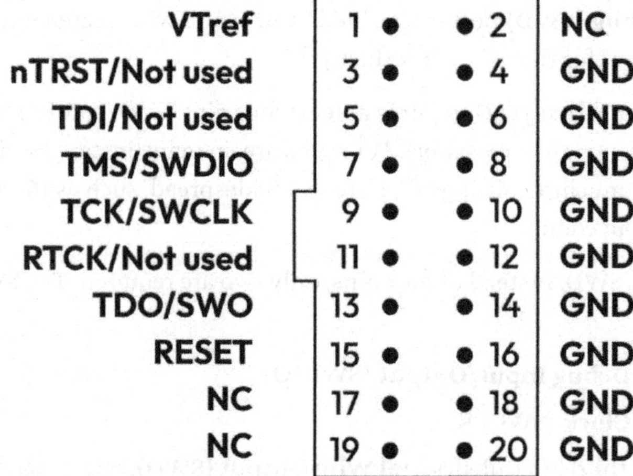

Figure 2.4: ARM standard JTAG connector pinout for JTAG and SWD

As you can see, SWD and JTAG are interchangeable on the same connector, so you can use the same design for both interfaces if needed.

The recommended, more modern connectors are on a smaller 0.05-inch pitch. There is also a smaller 10-pin variant called the **Cortex Debug connector**, as shown in *Figure 2.5*:

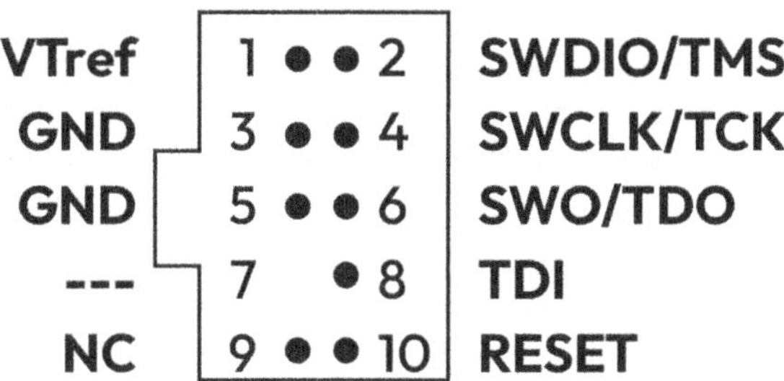

Figure 2.5: 10-pin Cortex Debug connector

In addition, we have a 20-pin variant called the **Cortex Debug+ETM connector** (also called the **ARM CoreSight 20-pin interface**, depending on which ARM manual you look at) [9], as shown in *Figure 2.6*:

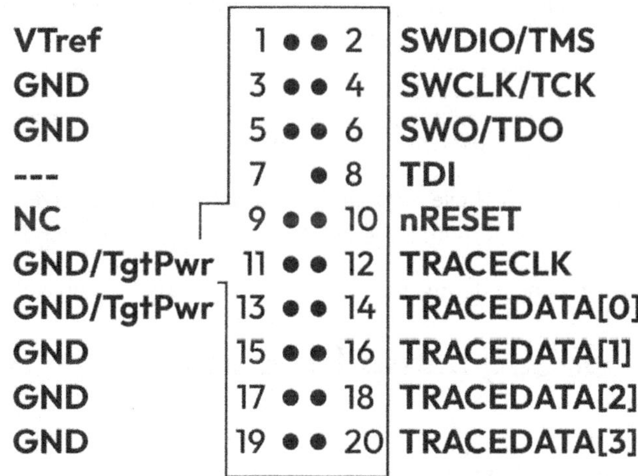

Figure 2.6: 20-pin Cortex Debug+ETM connector

The main reasons for the switch from the 0.1-inch pitch to 0.05-inch are size and cost reductions. Additionally, the Cortex Debug+ETM connector supports pin tracing, which will be explained in more detail in *Chapter 4*.

In the *SWD* and *JTAG* sections, we established what the corresponding SWD and JTAG pins are, but what about the other pins in the diagrams?

Table 2.3 explains all the extra pins that are not directly part of the debug interface itself:

Label	Description
NC	Stands for **Not Connect**. Simply, do not connect this pin.
GND	Electrical ground connection.
VTref	To be connected to the chip's power pin. Some debug probes determine the GPIO voltage level to use to drive the output pins from this.
TgtPwr	These pins can be used to supply a target supply voltage to the target to power either the target device alone or the whole board.
SWO	Stands for **Serial Wire Output**. It is an optional pin in the SWD interface that can be used for things such as `printf`-style debugging and tracing.
TRACECLK	Trace the clock signal of the parallel trace port interface.
TRACEDATA[0..3]	Trace data signals of the parallel trace port interface.

Table 2.3: Additional pin descriptions

Depending on whether and how these extra pins are utilized, they can give access to additional valuable debug and trace features, which we will learn more about in *Chapter 4*.

Next, we will learn how having a debug setup available can be extremely valuable.

How does a debug setup fit in your development workflow?

Let's assume that you already have an automated build system running that produces your output binary file. You maybe even have a way to automatically program the target device and run some unit tests, which can indicate whether they have passed or failed.

How would you analyze a test failure?

One approach would be to simply look at the problematic code part that failed the test and try to do a static analysis. While it is definitely a valid strategy that will yield results in many cases, it is not really very fast or flexible.

Another way would be to analyze the system log and see whether you can spot anomalies, which would bring you back to the approach before, where you do a static analysis on the problematic code around the affected log message.

Again, such setups will already catch and solve many bugs. But what if I told you that you were already debugging all along?

Yes, the approach is not very dynamic or modern, but you are actively using debugging techniques to systematically analyze an (ideally) reproducible problem.

But what if we could make it dynamic? What if we could alter and analyze the system state in real time?

That is what the main benefit of a proper debug setup is.

The wonderful thing is that you are probably already using the debug port of your target device to program it and control the test execution. So, why not also use it for debugging?

Yes, no one really wants to do debugging, as this usually means that the code you wrote is not executing as expected and probably has a bug somewhere. But why not use the tools that you have at hand to make the bug hunt as convenient as possible?

It is not even necessary to use all of the debug features that are theoretically available in your setup. Just using the basics will go a long way and make your life as an engineer significantly easier, so you can focus more of your time on creating new things instead of fixing existing legacy code.

Some of the benefits of a debug setup include the following:

- Faster issue resolution
- Consistent reproduction environment
- Immediate feedback loop
- Extended test coverage
- Reduced manual intervention
- Easier requirement fulfillment for certification

And best of all, as we have learned, a debug setup can be very budget-friendly. Most of today's embedded debug tools can be automated via the command line and thus be easily integrated into existing **Continuous Integration (CI)** setups.

Additionally, many modern debug probes can even be accessed remotely, so your target device and debug setup can be across the globe.

To finalize this chapter, here are my recommended best practices when getting started with a new project:

- Set up your version control system
- Get your build system up and running
- Set up your test framework and write tests alongside your source code
- Implement CI/CD pipelines
- Set up your software deployment channel(s)
- Set up post-deployment monitoring

Depending on the project size, some of the steps can be omitted. But don't forget: every large project once started small, and later in the project's life cycle, resources are often tied up.

Still not convinced? We will look at the debug features and techniques available today in the upcoming chapters.

Summary

In this chapter, we have learned about debugging and its significance in the embedded domain. The chapter outlined a typical debug setup, detailing essential components.

Additionally, we gained insights into the cost brackets associated with different debugging setups, helping us understand budget considerations when planning new projects.

Common debug interfaces were discussed, and we explained their functionalities and provided an overview of their respective advantages. Finally, the chapter illustrated how debugging integrates into existing development workflows, emphasizing its importance in ensuring efficient programming and problem-solving.

In the next chapter, we will take a deep dive into embedded debugging fundamentals. You will learn how to make the most of the hardware interfaces and debug setups introduced.

References

1. https://en.wikipedia.org/wiki/Debugging
2. https://en.wikipedia.org/wiki/Bug_(engineering)
3. https://en.wikipedia.org/wiki/Embedded_system
4. https://en.wikipedia.org/wiki/Bare_machine
5. https://en.wikipedia.org/wiki/Operating_system

6. Trinanjan, Nandi, Layered Operating System, 2025: `https://www.geeksforgeeks.org/operating-systems/layered-operating-system/`

7. Arm® Debug Interface Architecture Specification, 2022, ARM IHI 0031G

8. IEEE Standard for Test Access Port and Boundary-Scan Architecture, in IEEE Std 1149.1-2013, 13 May 2013

9. `https://documentation-service.arm.com/static/5fce6c49e167456a35b36af1`

Join our community on Discord

Join our community's Discord space for discussions with the authors and other readers: `https://packt.link/embeddedsystems`

3

Basic Debugging Features

When developing software, we are entering a domain where creativity, problem-solving skills, and patience to face various challenges are important virtues.

Debugging, while being an important piece of the puzzle, is not just about fixing errors; it is a systematic approach to understanding the nuances of expected code behavior and the application of various techniques to assist your curiosity and journey to find a solution to a particular problem.

This chapter will introduce the basic debug concepts and features that are available on most modern embedded devices that can assist you in that journey. As the reference platform, we will use a modern Arm Cortex-M85 device on an evaluation board with an on-board debugger. The chapter will show how to tackle certain issues with each feature and how it can be used to the developer's advantage.

The goal of the chapter is to provide you with the base skills and a toolset to be able to tackle the majority of software problems.

In this chapter, we will cover the following main topics:

- Debug states
- Disassembly
- Debug symbols
- Breakpoints
- `printf` debugging
- CPU registers
- Memory access and manipulation
- Call stack

Technical requirements

All of the code in the chapter can be found in the book's GitHub repository: `https://github.com/PacktPublishing/-Practical-Debugging-for-Embedded-ARM-Systems`

However, it is not required to follow along with the snippets and examples, as the purpose of this chapter is mainly to provide explanations and illustrate the concepts with screenshots.

General setup

My debug setup that I will reference consists of the following components:

- J-Trace PRO Cortex-M
- Renesas EK-RA8M1 board with an on-board debug probe
- Cortex-M trace reference board (based on ST STM32F407)
- SEGGER Embedded Studio IDE
- Ozone debug software
- SystemView
- Linux Mint 22.2 on host PC

Generally, I will have three configurations running and switch between them as needed.

Configuration 1 will be just the Renesas eval board with the on-board debug probe.

Figure 3.1: Renesas EK-RA8M1 board

The only connection between the host PC and this board is via a micro-USB cable connected to the connector labeled **J10 (DEBUG1)**. This will handle both power delivery and debug connection.

Configuration 2 will be the J-Trace PRO with the Renesas board.

The J-Trace PRO is plugged into the Cortex Debug+ETM connector (labeled **DEBUG3**), and the board is powered via the micro-USB port, as pictured in *Figure 3.2*. The blue cable at the top of the J-Trace PRO is plugged into the USB 3.0 port of the host PC, and the micro-USB cable is plugged into a USB power supply.

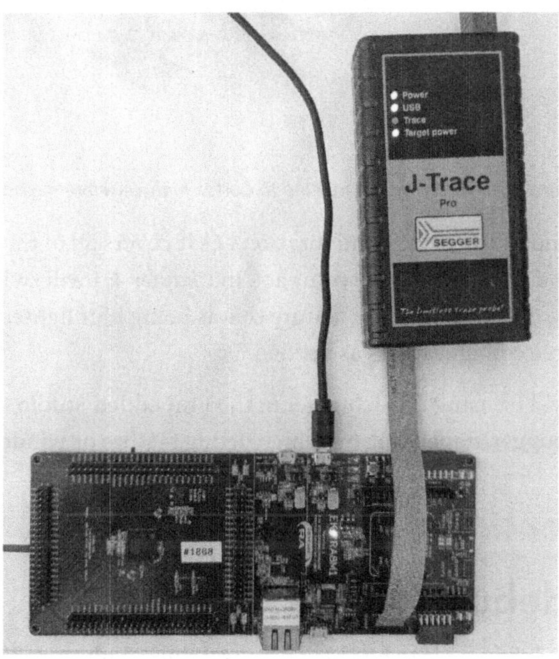

Figure 3.2: J-Trace PRO connected to the EK-RA8M1 board

Last but not least, configuration 3 will be the J-Trace PRO connected to the trace reference board. The board is powered through the debug probe via the debug connector, as mentioned in *Chapter 2*.

Figure 3.3: J-Trace PRO connected to Cortex-M trace reference board

In this chapter, I will mostly be using configuration 1 as it covers all of the basic debug features I want to showcase, and the setup is very compact. In *Chapter 4*, I will switch between configurations 2 and 3, depending on the feature that is being highlighted. *Chapter 5* will switch between all three configurations as needed.

As debug software, I will be using the debugger in the Embedded Studio IDE and the standalone Ozone debugger, depending on which debug feature or window will be highlighted.

Chapters 4 and *5* will also demonstrate the use of the software tracing tool called SystemView.

Controlling debug states

One key feature of any debugger is to be able to control the debug state of the target system. This section will explain what debug states are and how they can be used for debugging.

What are debug states?

Debug states refer to various operational conditions or modes that a target device can be in. The states help developers diagnose issues, optimize code parts, and ensure correct software functionality. The most common states are as follows:

- **Idle**: Target device is not being debugged and is free-running.
- **Debugging**: Target device is in debug mode. Some device features and clocks may behave differently to give better system insight during debugging.
- **Halted**: Target device is halted. No code is executed.
- **Stepping**: Target executes exactly one instruction or code line.

- **Reset**: Target is undergoing a reset process that resets the system into a predefined default configuration.
- **Sleep**: Target device is in a low-power state, conserving energy.
- **Faulted**: Target device has encountered a fault or exception.
- **Exited**: Target device has cleanly exited the `main` function and is now running the exit handler.

While most of these states are self-explanatory, we should talk a bit more about states: reset, sleep, stepping, and exited.

For this, we must understand the typical boot process of a free-running target device. Normally, after powering the target device, the core will start from a defined state as documented in the target device reference manual. If an application is programmed, the target device will try to run it. In some setups, there may be one or multiple boot stages where a bootloader is executed.

The boot process

A **bootloader** is a piece of software that runs before your main target application and can have multiple jobs. The main ones are initializing your system and loading your target application, usually called firmware. Other jobs that a bootloader may cover are firmware image verification, error handling of system faults, providing firmware update channels, self-tests, activation of security features, and boot channel selection.

As a rule of thumb, the more complex your hardware setup is, and the more complex your target application will be, the more likely it is that the bootloader will cover multiple or even all of these jobs at once. In really complex setups, there can even be multiple bootloader stages.

In principle, there are two bootloader variants: reprogrammable software and **read-only memory (ROM)** bootloaders.

A ROM bootloader will typically be found on a system that has no reprogrammable internal non-volatile memory (e.g., Flash), where an application could be stored to survive **power-on resets (PORs)**. So, the silicon vendor will have a dedicated memory ROM location that will have bootloader code burned permanently into the chip, so every time the chip powers up, it will first execute that ROM code (other names are stage 0 or first-stage bootloader).

In such setups, it is typical that the reference manual for the target devices will only show the device state after it has fully run through the ROM bootloader. Should you be able to halt the device via the debug interface before it has booted through, you might run into unspecified behavior.

Devices that have internal reprogrammable flash memory often do not have a ROM bootloader. Instead, the first code that the chip will execute will only be the code you have programmed for it. However, even in such setups, it can be beneficial to have your own software bootloader stage running before your main firmware.

Now that we understand how a system boots after power-on, what about a reset? How do you define it?

The ambiguity of resets

Generally, the goal of a reset is to restore the system to a defined system state, for example, after running into a system fault. We can achieve this by using hardware features of the chip to, for example, reset the whole device, including peripherals. Or we can choose to reset just the core itself. A reset can also be done manually via software by simply setting the CPU registers of the core to the initial values as they would be when booting after a POR.

All of these different approaches are valid reset types. The most common ones can be found in *Table 3.1*:

Reset Type	Description	Resets CPU Registers?	Resets Peripherals?
Power-on reset	Active when target device powers up	Yes	Yes
External reset	Triggered by external signal, for example, reset pin	Yes	Yes
System reset	Triggered by internal chip-specific signal	Yes	Yes
Core reset	Triggered by internal chip-specific signal	Yes	No
Software reset	Triggered through software	Implementation defined	Implementation defined
Debug reset	Triggered by debug probe	No	No

Table 3.1: Reset types

As we can see, there is not just one single reset type, and if you go deeper into reset strategies that combine multiple reset types, you will quickly notice that resets can become quite complex. This is especially the case with software resets where it is implementation-defined when the "stable" reset state is reached. Is it the first instruction after a pin reset? Or is it the last instruction of a ROM bootloader? What if the bootloader has multiple exit points—do we have the same system state guaranteed at each exit?

While a reset is a very powerful and valuable debug state and, in many cases, your only resource left to recover and debug faulty firmware, it is important to keep in mind that when people talk about "doing a reset," it can mean many different things.

For further reading, I recommend reviewing your device reference manuals and the Arm architecture and debug manuals.

System startup

Now that we have learned what a reset is, what happens next on the system?

On older "classic" setups that have no ROM bootloader, the case was relatively clear. On Arm Cortex-M, the first action a chip will do after a reset is to load up the initial **stack pointer (MSP)** value from memory address offset 0 and load the **program counter (PC)** value from address offset 4. That way, the initial program is loaded. The application is now executing the so-called reset handler routine, and we have a running system. What PC and SP are will be revealed later in the *CPU and peripheral registers* section.

On systems with a ROM bootloader, at first, the same thing happens. However, you usually retain full system control only after the bootloader has run through and initialized the system. What a ROM bootloader does and how many exit points it supports is implementation-defined and can become quite complex.

After exiting the ROM bootloader, you will typically end up in the secondary reset handler (or application startup) routine from the firmware image that you have programmed.

But what does such a reset handler routine do exactly? Or, in other words, what happens before the main function?

The first routine that is typically called from a reset handler is the system initialization routine. Its main job is to set up the target device for further operation, usually including the system clock initialization, peripheral clock initialization, vector table relocation, and external memory initialization.

The other part of the startup routine has to do with setting up the runtime environment. This is partially dependent on the programming language you are using, but in short, the runtime environment is needed for your application to function correctly. It will set up things such as your heap, global memory segments will be initialized to their predefined values or zeroed, constructors of global objects will be called (if, for example, C++ and global classes are used), and, last but not least, the application entry point will be called, which is usually the main function.

Now we are finally at the main, function, and we can start debugging the actual main application. Usually, a significant portion of the startup code is written in assembly, and the actual initialization steps are toolchain- and hardware-dependent. So, keep in mind that if you are moving between different toolchains, you will often have to fix your startup routines. But the good news is that the startup can be debugged normally, just like your main application. This brings us to the next debug state, which is "exited."

System exit

So far, we have learned what happens before the main function, but what happens if you reach the end of your application and simply return?

The answer is that it depends on your toolchain. A bare-metal system that calls the main function is typically not meant to ever return from that function.

On a program level, you would return to the original caller, which was your reset handler and its startup routine. But there is typically no more code to be executed.

Many toolchains have a dummy function that is invoked in such a case, which simply loops infinitely to avoid any unexpected issues. That function can also be modified to do some manual system cleanup and exit handling if required by your particular use case. One example use case might be if you run a **real-time operating system** (**RTOS**) and want to be able to shut down cleanly.

Stepping

The next debug state is **stepping**. The main idea of that feature is to enable step-by-step execution of the current instruction or code line. After each step, the CPU is automatically in a halted state again. That way, you can follow through your application step by step to analyze certain scenarios more precisely. Most debug software will offer different step scenarios via onscreen options, such as the following:

- **Step over**: Steps over the current instruction or code line. If it is a function call, it will execute the whole function and break on the next instruction after the function returns.

- **Step into**: For single instructions, it does the same as step over. If it is a function call, it will step into the function call so the program flow can be tracked a call depth deeper.

- **Step out**: Reverses step into by executing the application until the first instruction after the function returns.

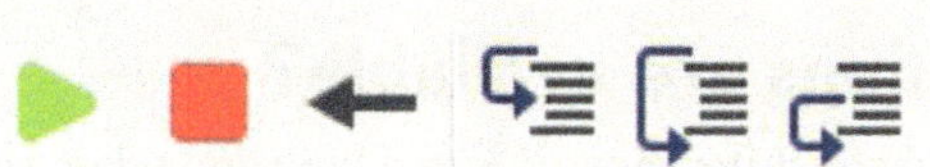

Figure 3.4: Example GUI buttons in the IDE (Embedded Studio) for state control. From left to right: continue, stop, restart, step into, step over, step out

Figure 3.4 also shows a green continue button that is used to start or continue code execution. Once pressed and the target device is running, that same button will change into a pause button, which can be used to halt target execution manually. The red stop button is used to stop the debug session completely.

While stepping is very effective and valuable, it is important to keep certain limitations in mind. First, depending on your hardware setup, it is possible that certain system timers might continue running even when your system is halted after a step. This might cause issues after resuming execution after a halt if the timer is coupled to some events, such as interrupts. So, be aware of this and configure your system accordingly.

The other thing to consider is that interrupts might not trigger as expected, as with each step, you might be halting any peripheral that would usually be free-running, so you might get unexpected system behavior when stepping compared to a free-running system. One such example is a watchdog interrupt that might not trigger. More on watchdogs will be covered in *Chapter 5*.

Sleep mode

The last debug state I want to focus on is **sleep**. A sleep or low-power mode will typically reduce the power draw of your system drastically, which makes it a very valuable tool, especially for battery-driven target systems. But there are some crucial drawbacks to consider.

The most obvious issue with sleep modes is that the debug unit on the core is typically also powered down, and thus, you no longer have control over the system via the debug interface.

Depending on the target device, this can be mitigated by enabling a sleep mode that keeps the debug interface active.

How many low-power/sleep modes are available on the device, and which chip components may behave differently in such scenarios, is implementation-defined. That's why enabling low-power or sleep mode can disrupt system logging and peripheral functions, cause loss of data in volatile memory, or create timing problems for events not configured for sleep mode. So, make sure to keep this in mind when using this mode.

What state transitions are available?

We have now learned about the different states and how and when they can be applied, and have even had a short introduction to the boot processes of an embedded system.

Now let's visualize these states in a diagram. The entry point of the state machine is typically a POR, which leads to the idle state where the application is free-running without being impacted by the debugger:

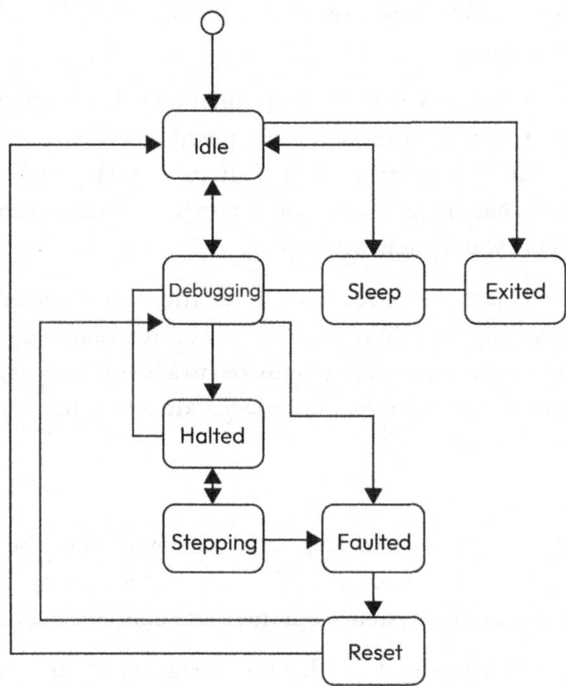

Figure 3.5: Diagram of a debug state machine

The different state transitions shown in *Figure 3.5* can be summarized as follows:

- **Idle to debugging**: Switch from an idle to a debug state and vice versa.
- **Idle to sleep**: Application goes to sleep while free-running. May wake up and return to an idle state.
- **Idle to exited**: Application runs through and returns from the main function.
- **Debugging to sleep**: While running in debug mode, the device enters sleep mode.
- **Sleep to exited**: After waking up from sleep, the device exits the main function.
- **Debugging to halted**: Occurs when execution is paused for step operations.
- **Halted to debugging**: Resuming execution.
- **Debugging to faulted**: Transition if a fault occurs during execution.
- **Halted to stepping**: Transitioning to step over instruction or code line. Then returns to the halted state.
- **Stepping to faulted**: Transition if a fault appeared during stepping.
- **Faulted to reset**: After recovery from a fault, the system may reset.
- **Reset to idle**: After a reset, the system returns to an idle state.

This is just one possible example. There are some additional state transitions that are possible under certain circumstances. But to keep things simple, we will leave this as is.

Practical approach

Now that we have learned about the different debug states, what can we practically do with them?

Let's look at some scenarios where the introduced states can be used.

Verifying program flow

The most obvious scenario is verifying the program flow of your target application by halting the application in a specific situation and stepping through your code.

As mentioned before, we can do so at either the source code or machine code level.

The following screenshot shows a scenario where we have startup code written in Arm Thumb assembly. We will learn what exactly that is in the following sections.

```
• Reset_Handler()                                        ⬦ ◆ ◆ ▶ ■ ← ⬚⬚⬚⬚ ∞ ⬚⬚
    154   #endif
    155   #ifdef __VECTORS_IN_RAM
    156           ldr     R1, =__vectors_ram
    157   #else
    158           ldr     R1, =__vectors
    159   #endif
    160           str     R1, [R0]
    161   #endif
    162   #if !defined(__SOFTFP__) && !defined(__NO_FPU_ENABLE)
    163           //
    164           // Enable CP11 and CP10 with CPACR |= (0xf<<20)
    165           //
⇨  166           movw    R0, 0xED88          // CPACR
▸   167           movt    R0, 0xE000
▸   168           ldr     R1, [R0]
▸   169           orrs    R1, R1, #(0xf << 20)
▸   170           str     R1, [R0]
    171   #endif
    172           //
    173           // Call runtime initialization, which calls main().
    174           //
▸   175           bl      _start
    176
```

Figure 3.6: Example Thumb assembler startup code

The yellow arrow shows the instruction that will be executed on the next step. You can find a live demonstration of stepping over the startup code in *Video 3.1*.

To access the videos in this chapter, go to `https://packt.link/tH1I2`, or scan the following QR code:

For completeness, the following screenshot shows a scenario where we step through C source code.

Figure 3.7: Example C source code being debugged

You can find a live demonstration of stepping over this source startup code in *Video 3.2*.

To access the videos in this chapter, go to `https://packt.link/tH1I2`, or scan the following QR code:

Testing correct reset behavior

Another important scenario is testing the correct reset behavior. By generating various reset types, we can verify whether our system behaves as expected when resetting it.

Most debuggers will also be able to stop at the first instruction, giving you the opportunity to debug step by step through your whole system startup or bootloader right from the beginning.

In some cases, you need to be able to stop after a ROM bootloader say by instrumenting your startup code. Such a feature might not be available with all debug probes. So if you are looking to debug a system that is in the valid state only after the ROM bootloader has executed, make sure to look for a debug probe that supports a method to achieve this.

Testing sleep mode entry

With control over the debug states, we can also debug whether our routine for sleep mode entry is behaving as expected. We can do that by simply stepping over the sleep mode entry instruction.

To enter sleep mode and test it on the Arm Cortex-M, the procedure is typically as follows:

1. Configure interrupts and low-power registers as required (target device-specific).
2. If possible, choose a configuration where the debug port stays active during sleep.
3. Enter sleep mode via a **wait for event (WFE)** or **wait for interrupt (WFI)** instruction [1].
4. Verify sleep or low-power mode entry by, for example, doing a power measurement or having some optical indicator, such as an LED that would only blink in an idle state.

As the names of the sleep mode entry instructions imply, a sleep or low-power mode on an Arm Cortex-M system relies on event handlers or interrupts that are triggered either externally, for example, via some hardware pin, or internally, via a timer.

Please note that you will have to configure at least one wake-up condition for your system or it will stay in sleep mode indefinitely. Also, should you be debugging your application and your debug connection is suddenly breaking up, it might be a strong indicator that you are putting your target device into sleep mode without realizing it.

That can specifically happen if you are using third-party code parts that you did not write yourself to bring up the project faster.

So, be aware of your sleep mode setup.

System state verification

By having control over your system, you can verify that it is in its expected state at any time. You can check memory regions, variable values, CPU registers, and many more.

The following sections will go into more detail on these concepts.

As an example, let's consider the following scenario.

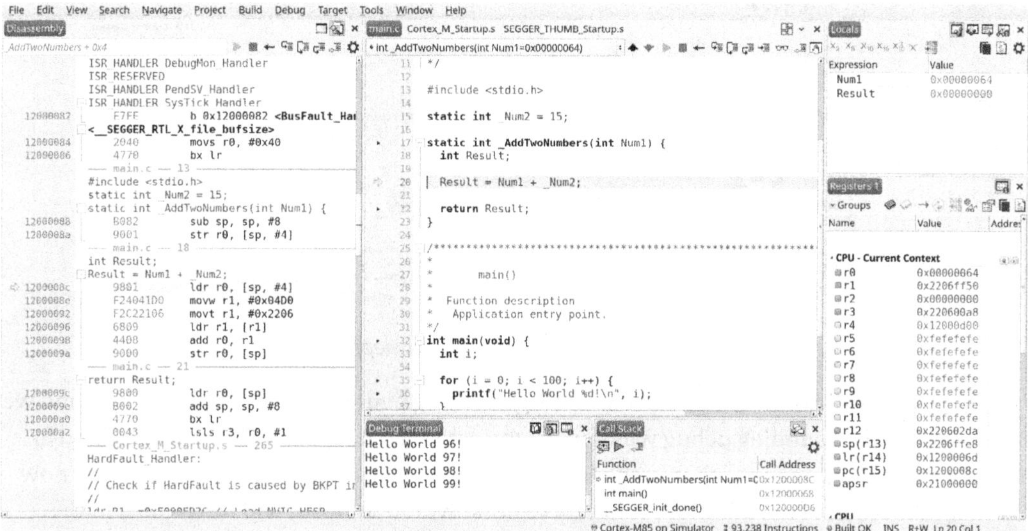

Figure 3.8: Example scenario before stepping

We have sample C code that is actively being debugged in Embedded Studio. The current system state is halted. We will step over *code line 20*. The code line simply adds the Num1 and _Num2 variables. One is a local variable within a function, and the other is a static variable that is accessible in the file's scope. To distinguish their scopes, the static variable has an underscore in its name.

Let's see what happens now if we step over that line.

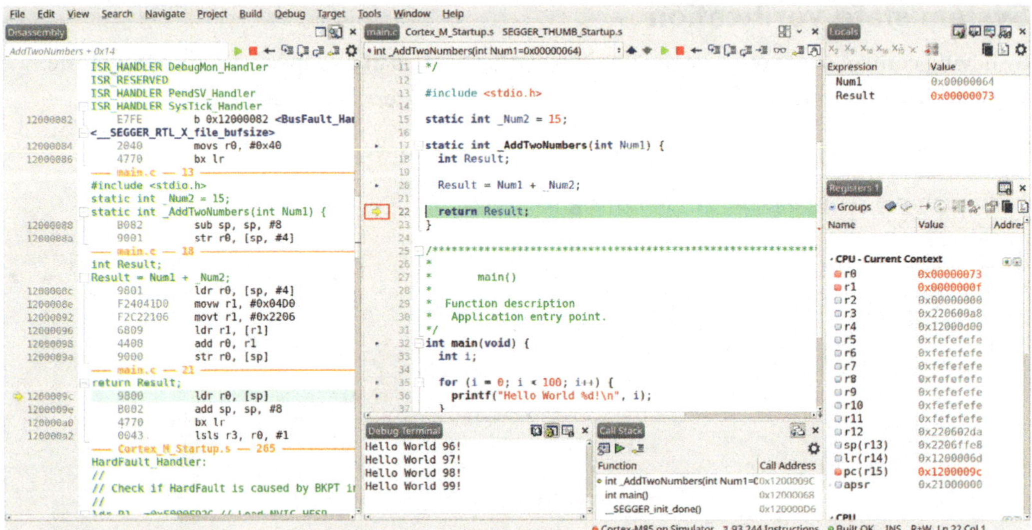

Figure 3.9: Example scenario after stepping

The yellow arrow (circled with a red box in the preceding figure) is now in the next line, and we see that in the surrounding debug windows, some data has changed, which is highlighted in red. For example, we can see that in the **Locals** window, the value for the **Result** variable now contains the result of the addition. What these other windows mean will be clarified in the following sections.

Disassembly

This section will discuss assembly code and how a so-called disassembly can help you to find out what exactly is happening on your target device.

Assembly is a low-level programming language that is closely related to machine code. It uses symbols and mnemonics to represent machine code instructions and to make it more understandable for humans than raw machine code.

Each computer architecture comes with its own set of assembly instructions, making assembly code not very portable.

Arm Cortex-M target devices support the Arm **instruction set architecture (ISA)**. In this book's examples, we will use Armv7-M and Armv8-M, which are both 32-bit architectures. The standout feature of these devices is the Thumb-2 instruction set, which combines 16-bit and 32-bit instructions for optimal performance-to-code size ratio, single-cycle execution for most instructions, and support for deterministic hardware interrupts via a vector table [1][2].

What is a disassembly?

A **disassembly** is a layer that translates the machine code back to human-readable assembly code. The idea is to enable reading binary data from a target device's memory and running it through the disassembler. By knowing the instruction set of the target device and the mode it is booting from, we can reverse-engineer the original assembly code that was generated by the compiler.

An example can be seen in *Figure 3.10*.

Figure 3.10: Machine code versus disassembly

On the left, we can see the raw machine code in a specific memory section, and on the right, we see the disassembled assembly code.

If the disassembler also has the source code info from the original binary at hand, it can even reference the source code to the disassembled instructions. This additional information can be referenced from debug symbols, which will be addressed in the *Debug symbols* section.

Specifics to consider with Arm Cortex-M

Arm has released various instruction sets over the years for their numerous chip architectures. A rough overview of the most common ones can be found in the following list:

- **ARM**: The original Arm 32-bit instruction set. Cortex-A and R architectures have kept backward compatability to this day.

- **Thumb**: The first approach to a more condensed 16-bit instruction set for a lower memory footprint. Was discontinued with the Armv7-M architecture.

- **Thumb-2**: A combination of 16-bit and 32-bit instructions for the best trade-off between code speed and size.

- **A64**: 64-bit instruction extension for Armv8.

- **A32**: 32-bit instruction set for Armv8.

- **NEON**: Multimedia instruction set for fast data processing.

- **Jazelle**: Support for native Java bytecode execution (barely supported by modern Arm chips, for example, Armv7 and later).

- **ARM cryptography extensions**: Instruction extension for boosting cryptographic operations.

On Armv7-M and Armv8-M, only Thumb-2 is available [1][2].

All Arm instruction sets are a **reduced instruction set computer (RISC)** tailored for resource-constrained environments such as embedded systems, where we still try to get the best performance per byte of code. So, code density and CPU cycle efficiency are key factors.

Practical approach

But how can we utilize the disassembly for debugging?

Let's take another look at the example from before with the small add function.

```
───── main.c ── 17 ──────────────────────
          static int _AddTwoNumbers(int Num1) {
12000090      B082          sub  sp, sp, #8
12000092      9001          str  r0, [sp, #4]
───── main.c ── 18 ──────────────────────
          int Result;
          Result = Num1 + _Num2;
12000094      9801          ldr  r0, [sp, #4]
12000096      F24041D0      movw r1, #0x04D0
1200009a      F2C22106      movt r1, #0x2206
1200009e      6809          ldr  r1, [r1]
120000a0      4408          add  r0, r1
120000a2      9000          str  r0, [sp]
───── main.c ── 21 ──────────────────────
          return Result;
120000a4      9800          ldr  r0, [sp]
120000a6      B002          add  sp, sp, #8
120000a8      4770          bx   lr
───── Cortex_M_Startup.s ── 147 ──────────
```

Figure 3.11: Arm disassembly of a function that adds two values

As we have the C source as well, the debugger can reference the corresponding source lines in the disassembly view for better context. The application is halted on the add function itself at the C source level. But at the assembly level, we can see that one C core line expands to six instructions starting at address 0x12000094.

The first instruction loads the first operand variable (Num1) from the stack to register R0. The next two instructions load the address for the location of the second operand. After that, the variable value for _Num2 is loaded from that location and stored in register R1. Finally, the two register values are added to each other, and the result is stored in register R0 and then stored on the stack.

If we combine this with the CPU registers, we can get very detailed system insights, and we can exactly follow the application and each operation that the **microcontroller unit** (**MCU**) will execute. That way, we can find potential bugs by verifying each instruction that is executed.

Another use case is attaching to an unknown application. Most debuggers will have an option to attach to an already-running system. We simply connect to the target device and can then take control over the black-box application that is running on it.

```
Disassembly
    0   08002DD8   F64E 5214    MOVW        R2, #0xED14
    0   08002DDA   5214         STRH        R4, [R2, R0]
    0   08002DDC   F2CE 0200    MOVT        R2, #0xE000
  - 0   08002DE0   5488         STRB        R0, [R1, R2]
    0   08002DE2   B002         ADD         SP, SP, #8
    0   08002DE4   4770         BX          LR
⇒ 0    08002DE6   E7FE         B           0x08002DE6
    0   08002DE8   F000 F822    BL          0x08002E30
    0   08002DEC   F64E 5088    MOVW        R0, #0xED88
    0   08002DF0   F2CE 0000    MOVT        R0, #0xE000
    0   08002DF4   6801         LDR         R1, [R0]
    0   08002DF6   F451 0170    ORRS        R1, R1, #0xF00000
    0   08002DFA   6001         STR         R1, [R0]
    0   08002DFC   F7FD F9C4    BL          0x08000188
    0   08002E00   B580         PUSH        {R7, LR}
    0   08002E02   2001         MOVS        R0, #1
    0   08002E04   F001 F866    BL          0x08003ED4
    0   08002E08   F240 70FC    MOVW        R0, #0x07FC
    0   08002E0C   F2C1 0000    MOVT        R0, #0x1000
    0   08002E10   6801         LDR         R1, [R0]
    0   08002E12   3101         ADDS        R1, #1
    0   08002E14   6001         STR         R1, [R0]
```

Figure 3.12: Disassembly window after attaching to the target device

Figure 3.12 shows the disassembly after this attach attempt and halting the device execution. We are now halted at address 0x08002DE6. We know what target device we are debugging by simply looking at the chip and looking up its reference manually. That way, we can already tell whether this code part is running in Flash or RAM. We also have access to the CPU registers and can now try to understand and reverse-engineer the target application that is running on the chip without ever having seen the original source code. We can also dump the firmware and try to decompile it with specific tools to try to reverse-engineer the original source code.

As we can see, by having control over a target system and access to a disassembler, we can already get very detailed system insights.

Debug symbols

This section will introduce you to the topic of debug symbols and why they are important to get a complete picture of the application that is being debugged.

What are debug symbols?

As we have already established, the application running on the target device is raw machine code that is not human-readable. With a disassembler, we can translate that machine code to assembly to get a better understanding of the application that is running on the device.

But what about the high-level programming language that we used to write the original source code? What about the original variable and function names, array sizes, string references, and many more details that are used in our high-level programming language to depict the program's logic?

That is where **debug symbols** come into play.

Debug symbols describe the originally compiled source code and map the machine code to their corresponding line numbers. Together with the original source code files, we can now reference the compiled machine code to the original source code. Along with a debugger that can interpret this information, we can now debug our application in the original source code files and have a better understanding of the intended program flow.

There are several different debug symbol standards and file formats. The dominant standard for debug symbols for embedded systems is **DWARF**. The most common file format is **Executable and Linkable Format (ELF)**. Yes, the names are medieval fantasy-inspired, because sometimes names can be funny as well as pragmatic!

Most code these days is generated by open source toolchains such as **GNU Compiler Collection (gcc)** or Clang. There is an enormous tool ecosystem around these toolchains, and these days, they produce quite the competitive output in terms of code size and speed, which are especially important on embedded target devices.

But there are also specialized proprietary toolchains that usually optimize the code even further and provide a more advanced feature set than their open source counterparts. The main reason is that the named open source toolchains are not created only with embedded systems in mind, so they may have more overhead than a toolchain designed specifically for one specific microchip architecture [3].

The biggest benefit of such proprietary toolchains is usually that you will be able to squeeze significantly more code into the same resource-constrained microchip. Or, on systems where, rather than the memory, the limited battery power is the constraint, with higher optimization, the code is executed more efficiently, saving precious energy. Additionally, you typically have a dedicated support channel and support contracts, so it is significantly easier to get quality help from the developers of the toolchains.

A potential drawback is that some proprietary toolchains will use proprietary debug symbols. That will greatly limit which debug software you can use later to reference the debug symbols to your source code. So, you might be stuck with the proprietary toolchain vendor in terms of additional tooling, for example, for debugging. But that is not the case for all available proprietary toolchains.

What should be considered in a toolchain setup?

Now that we know what debug symbols are, let's see what potential pitfalls are when building your application with a toolchain.

As you probably already know, there are different build settings and options that can be passed to your toolchain components, such as the linker, compiler, and assembler.

But not all settings will yield beneficial results when trying to debug an application. In many instances, there might even be a trade-off.

For reference, let's look at the compiler optimization options of the GNU compiler for Arm. The following options are available [4]:

- **-O0**: Optimization is disabled. Fastest compilation time, primarily for debugging purposes.
- **-O1**: Basic optimization that improves performance without significantly increasing compile time.
- **-O2**: Moderate optimization. Enables a range of optimizations, including inlining, loop unrolling, and strength reduction.
- **-O3**: High-level optimization. Includes all -O2 optimizations plus additional aggressive optimizations, such as vectorization.
- **-Os**: Optimizes for code size. Similar to -O2 but excludes optimizations that increase code size.
- **-Ofast**: Disregards strict standards compliance. Enables all -O3 optimizations and adds optimizations that may be unsafe. The goal is maximum performance at all costs.

- **-Og**: Optimizes for debugging. Provides a good balance between optimization and debuggability.
- **-Oz**: Optimizes aggressively for size over speed. Similar to -Os.

There are additional options and other tools in the toolchain, such as the linker, which can optimize further, but let's stick with the -O options for the compiler for now.

As we can already deduce from the naming and description, not all optimization levels are equally suitable for debugging. It is recommended to use -O0 and -Og. These optimization levels will ensure that the debug symbols match the machine code and thus the application can be debugged as expected.

But what happens if you choose higher optimization levels?

The main issues that can appear are the following:

- Higher compilation time
- Difficulties when debugging
- Over-optimization, leading to behavior change such as unexpected timing

As this is a book about debugging, we will focus on that issue.

With code optimization low or off, we have high alignment of the produced machine code and the source code reference. The debug symbols are unambiguous, and a debugger will show the program flow as expected when debugging.

Practical approach

Let's use the application from *Figure 3.8* of a simple add function. If the code is built with the compiler set to use debug-compatible optimization levels, everything is fine, and when stepping through the function, it behaves as intended by the developer, and the program flow is just as composed in C.

But what happens if we use -O3, for example?

```
main.c  Cortex_M_Startup.s  SEGGER_THUMB_Startup.s
• int main()
17  static int _AddTwoNumbers(int Num1) {
18      int Result;
19
20      Result = Num1 + _Num2;
21
22      return Result;
23  }
24
25  /*********************************************************************
26   *
27   *        main()
28   *
29   *  Function description
30   *    Application entry point.
31   */
32  int main(void) {
33      int i;
34
35      for (i = 0; i < 100; i++) {
36        printf("Hello World %d!\n", i);
37      }
38      i = _AddTwoNumbers(i);
39      do {
40        i++;
41        _Num2++;
42      } while (1);
43  }
```

Figure 3.13: Debug view after code optimization

The first thing that we notice is that the code size has changed. Initially, for `main.c`, we had 138 bytes for the code section and 21 bytes for the data section. After building with optimization level -O3, the code section drops to 66 bytes while the data section stays the same. So, there is quite a significant difference. The other thing is that there are now fewer arrows next to the C code lines. Before, we had an arrow at each code line. Now, there are only a couple. These arrows indicate which source code line the compiler has generated actual machine code for. As we can see, the whole `_AddTwoNumbers()` function is simply completely omitted.

The reason is simply that we told the compiler to optimize the code as harshly as possible, and for the compiler, it made no sense to include this function as the result of the calculation is not used later on, and it is even pre-determined at compile time. So, if the task is to optimize as harshly as possible, such code becomes useless in the eyes of the compiler.

Keep this in mind when structuring your application.

Another common toolchain pitfall is using variables such as constant strings that are defined globally but not used anywhere in your application. Often, such variables will be used to signal to a bootloader that the firmware that you are loading is valid. However, depending on the toolchain settings, it is possible that this data will be removed from the final binary file that is flashed to the target device, and thus your application will suddenly not boot. So, make sure that your toolchain settings fit your project scope.

But back to debug symbols.

Let's take a look at the good old Dhrystone benchmark application.

```
SEGGER_dhry_1.c

 74     /* Main and Proc_0 in the Ada version                    */
 75 {
 76          One_Fifty           Int_1_Loc;
 77   REG    One_Fifty           Int_2_Loc;
 78          One_Fifty           Int_3_Loc;
 79   REG    char                Ch_Index;
 80          Enumeration         Enum_Loc;
 81          Str_30              Str_1_Loc;
 82          Str_30              Str_2_Loc;
 83   REG    int                 Run_Index;
 84   REG    int                 Number_Of_Runs;
 85
 86     /* Initializations */
 87
 88     Next_Ptr_Glob = (Rec_Pointer) malloc (sizeof (Rec_Type));
 89     Ptr_Glob = (Rec_Pointer) malloc (sizeof (Rec_Type));
 90
 91     Ptr_Glob->Ptr_Comp                      = Next_Ptr_Glob;
 92     Ptr_Glob->Discr                         = Ident_1;
 93     Ptr_Glob->variant.var_1.Enum_Comp       = Ident_3;
 94     Ptr_Glob->variant.var_1.Int_Comp        = 40;
 95     strcpy (Ptr_Glob->variant.var_1.Str_Comp,
 96             "DHRYSTONE PROGRAM, SOME STRING");
 97     strcpy (Str_1_Loc, "DHRYSTONE PROGRAM, 1'ST STRING");
 98
 99   | Arr_2_Glob [8][7] = 10;
100           /* Was missing in published program. Without this state-
```

Figure 3.14: Dhrystone benchmark source code

The application starts by setting some pointers. Normally, if we step over these code lines without compiler optimization, they will be executed line by line. Take a look at *Video 3.3* and *3.4* to see what will happen if we turn the compiler optimization level to the maximum.

To access the videos in this chapter, go to `https://packt.link/tH1I2`, or scan the following QR code:

Video 3.3 shows the expected program flow. There are no unexpected jumps between lines 91–94 as there are only variables being set, and no functions are being called. In the disassembly window, we can see the corresponding machine code for each C source line; everything lines up nicely, and the debug symbols can be clearly mapped to the instructions.

However, in *Video 3.4*, the situation suddenly changes.

As we can see, the debug cursor suddenly jumps backward when stepping, only to jump forward again.

If we look at the corresponding disassembly and its mapping, we can see that the generated instructions for the same source code look vastly different now, and the debugger can no longer perfectly map each instruction to the debug symbols to get the expected code flow as before. So, we get this seemingly erratic behavior.

Such effects can happen with high levels of optimization, so you should be aware of that.

Nonetheless, without debug symbols, we would only have the machine code and a disassembly to debug with. So, it is always a good idea to let your toolchain generate the debug symbol files even with higher compiler optimization levels actively.

In summary, we have learned what debug symbols are, how they can be used to gain deeper knowledge of the system that is being analyzed, and what needs to be considered when dealing with code optimization on the toolchain level.

Breakpoints

This section will delve into the topic of breakpoints. We will learn what they are and how invaluable they are for any debug approach.

What are breakpoints?

Breakpoints are specific points in a program where code execution is intentionally stopped. This allows the developer to inspect specific code areas and verify the system's state.

They are a very valuable and flexible resource for debugging in general.

In host PC environments, we usually have an infinite number of breakpoints available to us, but as always, on embedded systems, things are a bit different. Host environments have the advantage that usually, the executed application code is fully loaded into RAM, which is volatile memory and thus easily readable and writable. When you set a breakpoint, for example, in an IDE, the debugger will replace the instruction in RAM at that position with a so-called breakpoint instruction. If the processor hits such a breakpoint instruction, it will immediately stop further code execution and wait for further commands from the debugger.

On the next debug-continue or step over, the original instruction will be written back to the location where the breakpoint was, and the code will work as before.

As we can do this for any location in RAM, we have unlimited breakpoint locations.

Available breakpoint types

Generally, we differentiate between hardware and software breakpoints.

We refer to breakpoint instructions in memory as software breakpoints. As we learned previously, in RAM, we can place as many breakpoints as needed with a debugger, even on embedded target devices.

But as established at the beginning of this chapter, many embedded systems execute parts of their code from non-volatile memory such as Flash, where breakpoint instructions usually can't be inserted as easily. In such cases, we rely on so-called hardware breakpoints.

Hardware breakpoints are a special variant of breakpoints that utilize CPU architecture-specific debug registers, which can be used to configure memory addresses and trigger conditions to set breakpoints in any memory location without needing to modify the executed code.

That includes Flash memory, and thus, hardware breakpoints are a valuable feature for embedded debugging.

But there is a catch. The number of hardware breakpoints is limited. Modern Arm Cortex-M devices typically have between 4 and 6 such breakpoints.[5]

While this is sufficient for many scenarios, it would be better if we could set as many breakpoints in non-volatile memory (e.g. Flash) as we can in volatile memory (e.g. RAM).

There are debug probes available on the market that implement a specific variant of software breakpoints that can also function in non-volatile memory. These are usually called "unlimited" or "infinite" Flash breakpoints. So, this might be something to look out for when searching for a new debug probe.

As mentioned before, in addition to introducing a break when a specific memory address is reached, hardware breakpoints can be used to impose additional trigger conditions. Hardware breakpoints configured in such a way are usually called **data breakpoints** or **watch points**.

The following screenshot shows an example configuration window for data breakpoints where we configure the breakpoint to trigger on a specific static variable when it reaches a specific value:

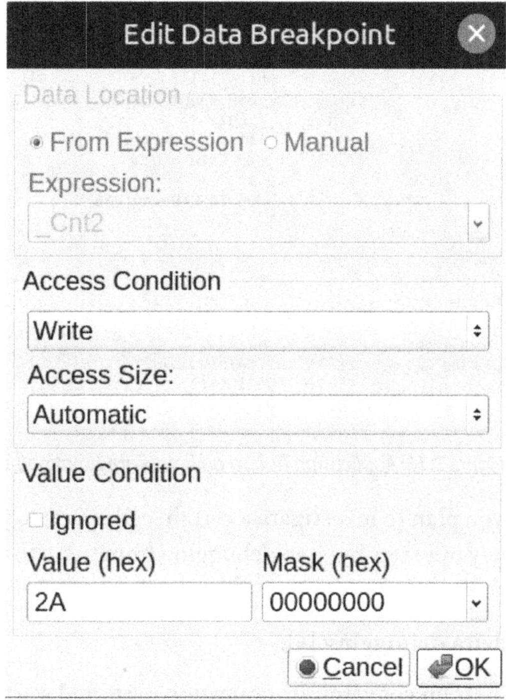

Figure 3.15: Ozone data breakpoint configuration window

The preceding example will break when the _Cnt2 variable reaches value 0x2A.

Which trigger conditions are available is usually implementation-defined by the hardware, but typically, you can set it to, for example, break on read, break on write, and break on certain value conditions.

Practical approach

Let's look at a couple of examples of how breakpoints can be utilized.

In the first example, we will set a simple hardware breakpoint on a Flash address that points to the start of a function. If we let the application run, it will at some point reach this code line and halt.

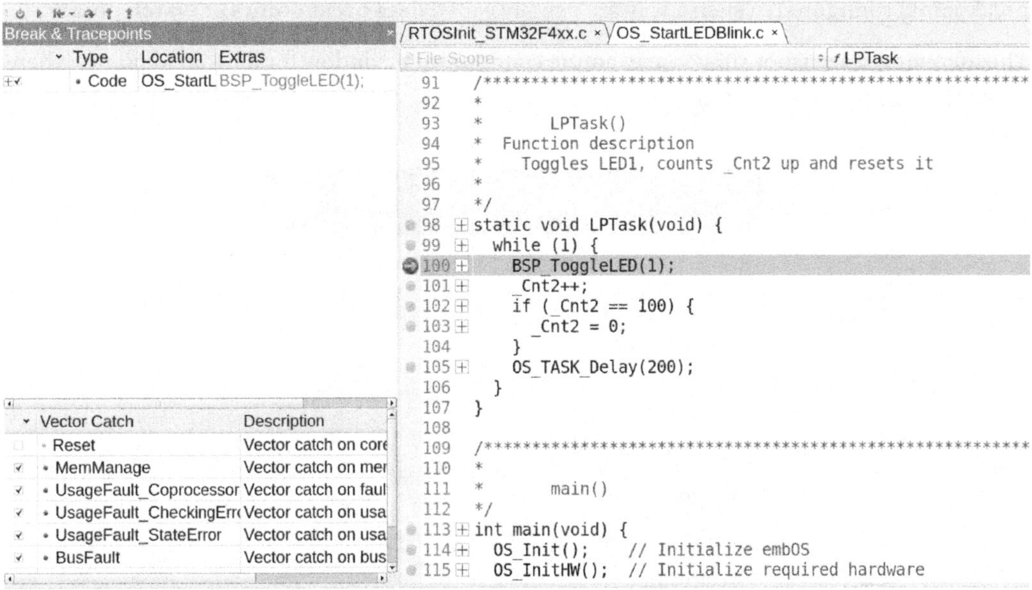

Figure 3.16: Application halted on hardware breakpoint

This approach is great if you plan to investigate a certain code part, so you can simply break at a specific location and carry out step-by-step debugging from there to check whether the code behaves as expected.

Another great benefit is **delta debugging** [6].

The idea is to set breakpoints on converging application parts and see which path the code will take in the current scenario. This can be useful if you are debugging source code that you are not completely familiar with but still want to narrow down where a specific bug might be coming from. Another scenario where this can be very helpful is if you are using function pointers in C but have not exactly mapped out which of the potential functions that are loaded might be called. By simply setting breakpoints in all potential candidates, you can quickly verify your code path without wasting a lot of time.

Data breakpoints, on the other hand, are most useful when trying to narrow down very specific bugs that only appear under very specific conditions. Let's assume we have some loop where multiple sensors are checked, and only a certain combination of sensor output values triggers a specific fault. Now, we could add debug code that checks this and use regular breakpoints, or we could simply use a data breakpoint with the specific condition, so we do not have to alter the application at all but can still catch the scenario where the code fails.

Now that we have learned what breakpoints are, which types are available, and how they can be utilized for debugging, let's move on to the next concept: logging.

Debugging with printf

In this section, we will learn how the classic approach of logging via printf is still one of our go-to debugging approaches. We will see how it holds up today, how it has evolved over the years, and how it can be used to our advantage.

What is printf?

printf is a C standard library function whose purpose is to print formatted text to some output interface or console. The principal idea of printf is pretty much available in every programming language. So, what is discussed in this section will apply to any programming language that is viable for embedded target devices and that has some sort of standard output function.

The standard definition of printf is as follows:

```
int printf ( const char * format, ... );
```

The function takes a string or char array as an input parameter, which can have format specifiers applied. The return value will output how many characters were written on success. On error, it will return a negative number, and depending on the library implementation, it will set additional error flags.

Functionally, the toolchain that is building your application will route the printf calls to a predefined interface where they will be displayed.

On host environments, the default output interface for printf is simply the console output of the caller.

On embedded systems, we typically do not have a console from a caller where we could print the string. Additionally, we must consider that we are usually on resource-constrained systems with little memory while trying to run real-time applications. So, we have to make sure that the interface for `printf` that is used uses as little memory as possible while at the same time being as non-intrusive to our system's execution as possible.

Which output interfaces are available?

The most common print interfaces on embedded systems are the following:

- **Universal asynchronous receiver-transmitter (UART)**
- **Serial wire output (SWO)**
- **Semihosting**
- **Real-time transfer (RTT)**

There can, of course, be custom solutions as well, but we will focus on the most prominent ones for Arm Cortex-M.

UART

UART is a bidirectional hardware communication protocol used for asynchronous serial communication. It is a two-wire system without a dedicated clock line, so the sender and receiver must agree on a baud rate and frame structure to be able to communicate. UART was first introduced in the 1970s and is a good and reliable option that is still widely used to this day.

The biggest benefits of UART are that it is very easy to bring up software and hardware-wise, it offers decent transfer speeds, it needs a reasonable number of pins, and it has proven itself over many decades.

The biggest drawback is that it is usually implemented in a blocking fashion, meaning that the rest of the target application must wait for the data transfer to finish, and depending on the size of the requested data transfer, this can take quite some time. On resource-constrained real-time systems such as microcontrollers, this may be a luxury that cannot be afforded.

In such scenarios, UART is not a viable print channel.

SWO

To fix some of the drawbacks of UART, Arm introduced the SWO pin and serial wire viewer protocol. The idea was to have a simple hardware-integrated output pin that can be used for data transfer from target devices to the debug software on the host PC with less overhead and higher speeds than UART. The bring-up software-wise was even simpler than UART as it is now a dedicated debug feature in the core.

Additionally, SWO allows doing some basic types of tracing, such as event and periodic PC sampling, which will be explained in more detail in *Chapter 4*.

But some of the drawbacks of UART remain, and we still see a noticeable impact on system performance.

Semihosting

As an honorable mention, I want to add **semihosting** to the list. It was defined by Arm in the 1990s, and the plan was to have a standardized debug channel between the target and host systems that can be used for various debug features known from host systems. It is still available on today's Arm Cortex devices and can be used for a plethora of things, such as the following:

- File operations on the host filesystem
- Terminal I/O operations, such as for logging
- Time functions to get time references to the target device from the host

The biggest benefit of semihosting is that it does not require any extra pins but simply utilizes the debug interface that is connected to the debug probe.

It suffers from similar limitations to UART in terms of system overhead. Additionally, while the host-like features, such as getting an accurate timing base or being able to access a full external filesystem, may sound good on paper, they are unfortunately not very useful in production code as it would require a debug probe and a host PC to be connected to the target device at all times. So, that scenario is only really viable when doing things such as unit testing, where you can store test data and test results directly on the host filesystem, for example.

The main benefit of semihosting is the I/O interface as it does not require extra pins and is always available on Arm devices.

RTT

Last but not least, I want to introduce RTT. It is a proprietary solution to the limitations of the interfaces above and is available with J-Link debug probes.

It takes advantage of a feature of Arm Cortex-M target devices, which is background memory access. That feature allows the debug probe to read the target device's memory while it is running.

To create an I/O channel between the host and target devices, we allocate RTT up and down buffers in our target system's RAM. The debug probe can access these buffers freely and thus exchange data with the target device while it is executing its firmware.

The following diagram shows the working principle of RTT.

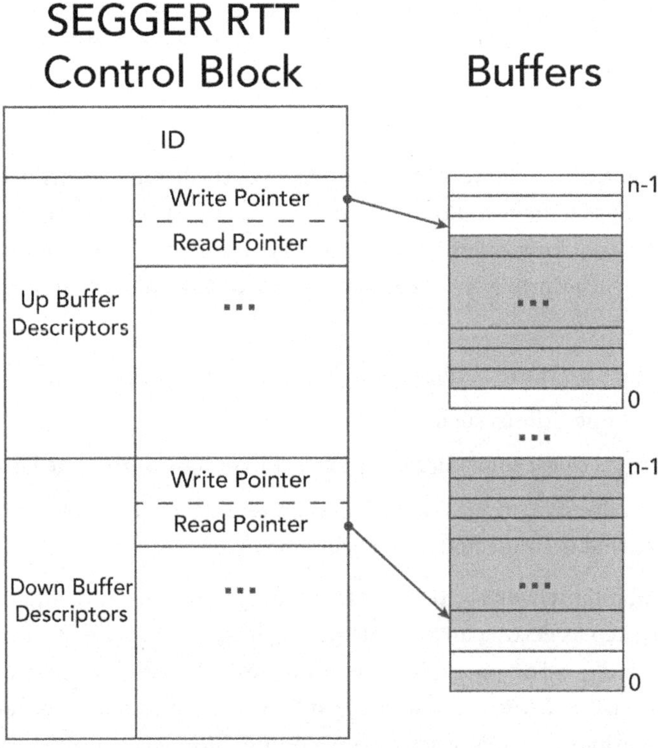

Figure 3.17: RTT buffer diagram

To use RTT in your firmware, simply add the RTT sources that are provided by SEGGER Microcontroller GmbH and call the corresponding RTT API functions instead of using `printf`. Most toolchains will allow rerouting your `printf` calls to alternative APIs such as RTT; that way, you do not have to replace the `printf` calls in existing applications.

While this approach does come with the drawback that some of the target device's memory is blocked by this feature, the advantages outweigh the negatives.

A big advantage is that no additional debug pins are needed for this to function. The regular JTAG or SWD interface is used. That way, very high data transfer speeds of >3 MB/s can be achieved. Additionally, compared to the other introduced `printf` interfaces, RTT only has minimal system impact on the application runtime, which can be seen in the following diagram:

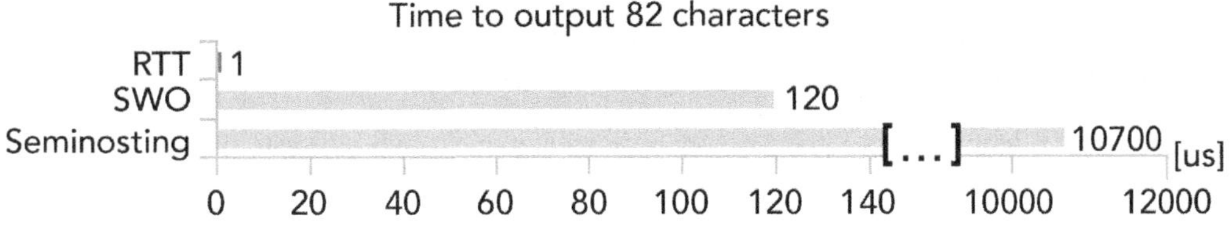

Figure 3.18: RTT speed comparison

So, whenever available, I strongly recommend using RTT as it allows you to use `printf` debugging even in systems with tight timing constraints.

Practical approach

Generally, `printf` can be used in various ways. For variable tracking:

```
float temperature = 23.5;
int humidity = 67;
printf("Sensor Reading: Temp = %0.1f°C, Humidity = %d%%\n", temperature,
humidity);
```

For error logging and other various logging tasks:

```
int error_code = 0x3F;
unsigned int memory_address = 0x20001000;
printf("DIAG: Error 0x%02X detected at memory location 0x%08X\n", error_code,
memory_address);
```

`printf` is a very versatile tool that can be used in many ways.

Each of the introduced print interfaces requires different kinds of preparation or initialization to make them available.

In the case of hardware interfaces such as SWO and UART, you will have to initialize the actual pins on the hardware and configure the underlying peripherals to send out the data as expected.

Semihosting, on the other hand, does not require any hardware-specific configuration but is instead triggered by the target application itself, and the debugger decides on target halt what action is requested by the target application by reading its CPU registers.

In the case of RTT, there are also no hardware initializations required. You simply add the RTT source files to your application, include the RTT header in your files, and use the RTT API. Or, if your toolchain allows it, you can reroute the `printf` call to the RTT API.

All in all, `printf` debugging is a great debug option even on embedded systems, and with modern interface variants such as RTT, it is even real-time-capable.

Now that we have learned all about the different `printf` interfaces and methods, let's take a closer look at CPU registers.

CPU and peripheral registers

This section will explain what CPU and peripheral registers are, what information they contain, and how they can be utilized for debugging.

What are registers?

Registers are small and fast storage locations within the CPU that can be used to store data, instructions, addresses, or special CPU state information.

The maximum register size is typically determined by the CPU architecture. A 32-bit system will usually have a maximum register size of 32 bits or smaller, for example, 16 bits or 8 bits. But as always, there can be exceptions to this rule.

We distinguish between CPU registers and peripheral registers.

CPU registers are required for the general operation of a CPU so it can do calculations, read/write to memory, and change the system state.

The most important CPU registers for an Arm Cortex-M85 are as follows:

- General-purpose registers R0–R12:
  - Used for arithmetic operations and data manipulation
  - Used to pass function parameters
- Stack pointer (SP/R13):
  - Points to the current top of the stack
- Link register (LR/R14):
  - Contains the return address after function calls
- Program counter (PC/R15):
  - Tracks the address of the next instruction to be executed

With these 16 registers, all conceivable programming tasks can be solved.

There are some additional CPU registers, such as special-purpose registers, floating-point registers, and control registers, which tell us more about the system state and can be used to trigger system state changes at will. But we will come back to some of these additional registers in later chapters.

Peripheral registers, on the other hand, are not crucial for the general operation of the system, but they describe the target device's peripheral space and make it available to configure a certain peripheral or carry out I/O operations on it.

Peripheral registers are memory-mapped and can thus be easily accessed via the target application.

The most common peripherals that you will find on Arm Cortex-M devices are UART, USB, **general-purpose input/output (GPIO)**, **analog-to-digital converter (ADC)**, Watchdog, and a hardware timer.

As which peripherals are available, how they are mapped, and what features they support is implementation-defined, Arm has invented a universal register description file format called **System View Description (SVD)**. These are XML files provided by silicon vendors for their particular device that describe all peripheral registers of the chip as documented.

Most modern debuggers are able to read this register format and make the information available to you while debugging, so you can get an even deeper system insight.

Practical approach

Now that we know what registers are, let's see how they can help us with debugging.

Let's check the different information that we can get from the CPU and peripheral registers.

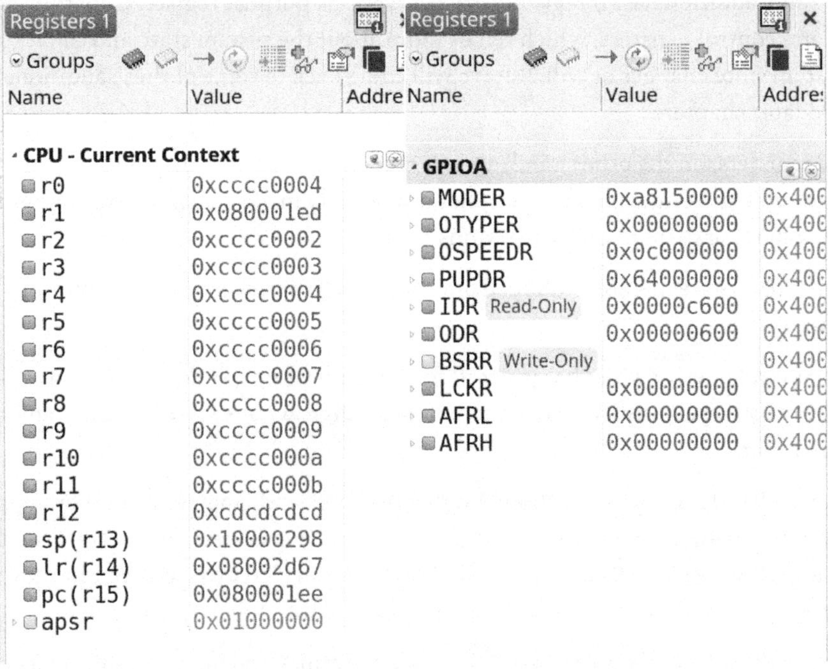

Figure 3.19: Register window view

On the left, we can see the CPU registers, and on the right, a peripheral group view for the GPIOA pin group on this target device.

How can this be used now for debugging? Let's cycle back to the example where we added two variables in *Figures 3.8* and *3.9*.

As we can see, with each step, we see the register window update and highlight the CPU registers that have changed compared to the previous instruction. The same works for highlighted peripheral registers as well.

Video 3.5 shows exactly how the registers change for each instruction that is executed.

To access the videos in this chapter, go to `https://packt.link/tH1I2`, or scan the following QR code:

> **Note**
>
> As a side note, you can also write registers via the register window. That includes the peripheral registers as well. With that feature, you can quickly try out configurations and state changes in your application without needing to change the source code and recompile the application each time.

Now that we have learned about CPU and peripheral registers and how they can be utilized for debugging, let's move on to the next topic: utilizing memory access for debugging.

Memory access and manipulation

This section will discuss system memory access and manipulation. We will learn about different memory types and how they can be accessed. We will then look at how memory access can be used for debugging.

What memory types are available?

Generally, we distinguish between volatile and non-volatile memory. However, there are also variants in between them. The main difference is that volatile memory is typically erased or becomes invalid after losing power, while non-volatile memory will keep its data integrity. Additionally, volatile memory can be easily erased and written at any time. There is also semi-volatile memory, which is a mixture of both properties, where the data is retained after power loss while at the same time keeping the benefit of being able to write to the memory at any time.

The following memory variants are typical for embedded systems:

Type	Description	Volatility
Tightly coupled memory (TCM)	Very fast storage that is used for time-sensitive application parts. In architectures other than Arm, it is also known as local memory or local storage.	Volatile
RAM	Fast and temporary storage for currently processed data.	Volatile
Non-volatile RAM (NVRAM)	Retains data after power loss. Slower and more costly than regular RAM, so only used on small areas for crucial data.	Semi-volatile
Flash memory	Electrically erasable and programmable memory storage. Retains data after power loss. Has limited erase cycles.	Semi-volatile
ROM	Non-programmable memory that retains data permanently.	Non-volatile
Programmable ROM (PROM)	ROM that can be programmed once after manufacturing.	Non-volatile
Erasable PROM (EPROM)	Can be erased via UV light. Reprogrammable multiple times.	Non-volatile
Electrically Erasable PROM (EEPROM)	Can be erased and programmed electrically.	Non-volatile

Table 3.2: Memory types

On most embedded target devices, you will at least find Flash and RAM, where Flash usually stores the firmware and RAM contains the stack and currently processed data.

Usually, these memory types are embedded in the chips and thus considered to be internal. But there are also variants where external memory is added on the PCB and connected to the MCU, for example, to expand storage or decrease cost or package size for the MCU. The main drawback of external memory is that accessing it is usually slower compared to internal memory, but the memory density is typically much higher in comparison.

How can they be accessed or manipulated?

Internal memory is normally memory-mapped to the data bus on the MCU, and thus the core can easily access the data via its CPU registers. However, for external memory, the story is a bit different. Here, we have to connect the external Flash or RAM chip to the MCU via pins.

There are several standardized communication protocols and pin interfaces to connect the external memory to the MCU.

The most common are **serial peripheral interface (SPI)** and **inter-integrated circuit (I^2C)**. To be able to access external memory, you will have to implement these protocols on your MCU.

Some microcontrollers might even have a peripheral that implements these protocols on the hardware level, so initialization is much simpler than doing everything from scratch; check out your device's reference manual to see whether a peripheral is available on your device.

Internal Flash is a bit different. For reading, it is memory-mapped and available via the internal data bus to the CPU, but manipulating it is not straightforward. For that, you usually have to write an application called a flash loader, which is loaded by your debug probe. The Flash loader then interacts with the on-board Flash controller, giving you access to erase and write functionality.

Practical approach

The main benefit of being able to read memory locations at any point in time is that we can very easily track variable values to get a better understanding of our current system and application state.

Another useful approach is to manipulate variable values directly while debugging. While the device is in a halted state, the local and global variable windows will display all available variables in the current scope.

Via a watch window, you can also single out certain important variables should you only want to track a specific subset of your global variables.

By simply clicking into the variable value fields, you can modify the value of that variable value, which will then be used by the target application instead of the original value. This can be used with any memory type if supported by your particular debug probe.

That way, you can test different code paths very quickly without needing to recompile the target application every time to change, for example, function parameters at a specific location that you are debugging.

We now have learned how memory access can be used to gain additional system knowledge on various memory types. Next up, we will look at the call stack.

Call stack

This section will explain what a call stack is, how it works on the Arm Cortex-M, and how it can be utilized for debugging.

What is a call stack?

To understand what a **call stack** is, we first need to understand how a stack works on microcontrollers. A stack is a data structure that operates in a **last in, first out** (**LIFO**) fashion. It is located in RAM and grows "backward" on the Arm Cortex-M architecture. That means that the initial top of the stack address will be higher than the top of the stack address of a filled stack.

The standard operations to add or remove data from the stack are called push and pop. On a microcontroller, the stack is mostly used to track function calls, local variables, and interrupt context handling.

A call stack is a visual representation of the function call order that was stored on the stack. On each function call, the function return address and optionally other CPU register values are stored on the stack, the so-called stack frame.

If you halt execution with your debugger and you are halted within a nested function call by doing a stack walk, the debugger can determine what the call order of the prior functions was.

Together with debug symbols, a debugger can additionally reference the corresponding source code.

Armv7-M architecture defines two types of stacks: the **main stack pointer** (**MSP**) and the **process stack pointer** (**PSP**). The MSP is the default stack used for ordinary bare-metal applications and interrupt handling. The PSP is usually utilized by the RTOS, which can use the second stack type for task management, as each task switch will typically push the current task context to the stack.

On Armv8-M, we also have the same stack types. Additionally, there are stack limit registers that can be configured to detect stack overflows, which will be covered in *Chapter 5*.

Practical approach

Here is a call stack of an embedded application that will read a measurement from a sensor that is attached to the MCU.

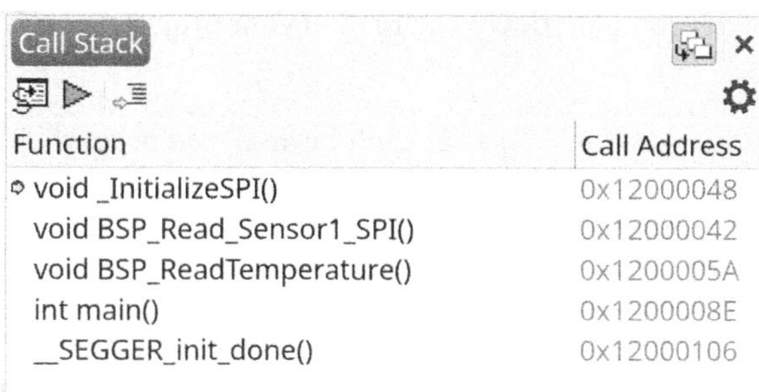

Figure 3.20: Callstack view

We can now see the call order of the current method, `_InitializeSPI()`. The order is from bottom to top. By clicking on one of the prior methods, the debugger will also show the corresponding source code reference, so it becomes very easy to follow the prior code execution path, which can be crucial when analyzing faults or exceptions.

In particular, when the debugging system crashes, the call stack can be a valuable resource to find out which methods have been called just prior to the crash. If you are lucky, you can then tell what caused the crash in the first place.

However, there are limitations to what a call stack can show you. Certain bugs may overwrite part of the system stack and thus potentially overwrite information about the function return addresses that are usually pushed to the stack for function returns. If that information is missing, the debugger can no longer reconstruct the program flow, and the call stack may remain empty. For such cases, instruction tracing can be used, which will be introduced in the next chapter.

The topic of crash analysis will be explored in more depth in *Chapter 5*.

Summary

We have now made it to the end of this chapter.

I hope I was able to introduce some new debugging features and concepts that inspire you to explore different approaches and methods for analyzing software problems.

We learned about important fundamentals, such as logging, breakpoints, and debug state control. We also dove into more situational features, such as memory manipulation, debug symbol analysis, and register operations.

These features are typically available with most embedded debug setups and are thus easily accessible. Should you be undecided about whether you want to spend the effort to get an embedded software debug set up and running to assist your development efforts, my recommendation is that you should definitely do it. The initial setup time dwarfs in comparison to the benefits you gain down the road in your project, specifically when you run into difficult bug types.

However, there will be bugs or scenarios that can't be analyzed properly just with the basic debug features. For such scenarios, more advanced debug features may be required, which will be introduced in the next chapter.

References

1. ARMv7-M Architecture Reference Manual: `https://developer.arm.com/documentation/ddi0403/latest`

2. Armv8-M Architecture Reference Manual: `https://developer.arm.com/documentation/ddi0553/latest/`

3. `https://www.segger.com/products/development-tools/embedded-studio/technology/tools/segger-compiler/`

4. GNU gcc, Options That Control Optimization: `https://gcc.gnu.org/onlinedocs/gcc/Optimize-Options.html`

5. Arm Cortex-M4 Processor Technical Reference Manual Revision r0p1: `https://developer.arm.com/documentation/100166/0001?lang=en`

6. Delta debugging: `https://en.wikipedia.org/wiki/Delta_debugging`

Get this book's PDF version and more

Scan the QR code (or go to packtpub.com/unlock). Search for this book by name, confirm the edition, and then follow the steps on the page.

Note: Keep your invoice handy. Purchases made directly from Packt don't require an invoice.

4

Advanced Debugging Features

In *Chapter 3*, we learned about various basic debug features, such as breakpoints, `printf` debugging, debug state control, usage of the call stack and disassembly for debugging, and much more. What these debug features and techniques all have in common is that they are usually readily available on modern embedded systems and are thus easily accessible.

However, in some instances, these features may not be sufficient to analyze a problem completely.

That is why, in this chapter, the focus will be on more advanced debug features that might have a more niche use case but are very valuable if extra system insight is needed.

In this chapter, we will cover the following main topics:

- Software and hardware tracing
- Live symbol tracking
- Power profiling
- RTOS awareness
- Monitor mode debugging

By the end of the chapter, you should be able to apply the introduced advanced debug techniques and features and be able to recognize when a specific technique may be required.

Technical requirements

This chapter is designed so that you theoretically do not need any software or hardware to follow along, as all scenarios and examples are accompanied by detailed explanations, screenshots, and videos.

But for completeness, for anyone who likes a more hands-on experience, the following hardware and software components were used for this chapter.

- J-Trace Pro Cortex-M
- Renesas EK-RA8M1 Board with on-board debug probe
- Cortex-M Trace Reference Board (based on ST STM32F407)
- SEGGER Embedded Studio IDE
- Ozone debug software
- SystemView
- Linux Mint 22.2 on host PC

All code in the chapter can be found in the book's GitHub repository: `https://github.com/PacktPublishing/-Practical-Debugging-for-Embedded-ARM-Systems`

Software tracing

We will begin with **software tracing**. In this section, we will learn what software tracing is, what typical methods are, and how they can be utilized most effectively.

What is software tracing?

Let's first define what tracing is, in general.

Tracing refers to recording and analyzing events that happen during a program's execution. There are various types of tracing, including event tracing, system tracing, and instruction tracing. This practice allows developers to gain insights into how their software operates, pinpoint errors, and enhance performance [1].

The most common technique for both event and system tracing is **logging**, a specific form of software tracing. In this method, the system periodically (and/or based on events) writes messages to a log file, which developers can review later.

A prime example of this is the system log found in Linux systems. However, event or system logs can also be generated in embedded systems, often using the `printf()` function from the C programming language.

Which methods are available?

As previously referenced, the most basic way of doing software tracing is simply by logging system messages (e.g., via `printf`). As we learned in *Chapter 3*, multiple I/O channels can be utilized on embedded systems for this.

Logging is very versatile and can be tuned exactly to fit your needs in regard to verbosity and logging frequency. It is also very portable, so if you have one log framework in place, you can port and reuse it easily in other projects as well.

One way of doing more sophisticated logging is to add the log calls to your application in a way that lets you reconstruct the program flow at a later time. This is called **code instrumentation**. Typically, you will also log timestamps, so you know the timing of each log entry.

But as we learned in *Chapter 3*, logging via `printf` is always intrusive, so we waste precious CPU cycles on the target hardware and, with some interfaces, even the limited memory that we have available to us. So how can we improve this?

We learned before that the interface itself is an important factor, and, for example, with RTT, we can make logging minimally intrusive.

What else can we do?

`printf` has the major drawback that the complete string formatting is done in the target application itself. In the realm of embedded systems, system memory is precious, and most full `printf` implementations are relatively large in size. So, what if we remove the whole formatting, and what if we do not even work with strings anymore, but instead encode the information efficiently on the target device so that the data being output to the host is reduced? That way, we can transfer much more data via the same debug interface bandwidth that is available to us, and at the same time, by doing the decoding on the host side, we do not waste precious cycles for target-side formatting.

Practical approach

Let's first look at a classic system log that was recorded with `printf`:

```
2026-01-12 08:00:01 - [INFO] - Device Booting Up
2026-01-12 08:00:02 - [INFO] - Wi-Fi Module Initializing
2026-01-12 08:00:05 - [INFO] - Wi-Fi Connection Established
2026-01-12 08:00:08 - [INFO] - Connecting to Cloud Server
2026-01-12 08:00:10 - [INFO] - Successful connection to Cloud Server
2026-01-12 08:00:12 - [INFO] - Sensor Module Activated
2026-01-12 08:00:13 - [INFO] - Set Sensor Polling Interval: 60 seconds
2026-01-12 08:00:15 - [DATA] - Temperature Sensor Reading: 24.5°C
2026-01-12 08:00:15 - [DATA] - Humidity Sensor Reading: 45.0%
2026-01-12 08:00:18 - [INFO] - Sending Data to Cloud
2026-01-12 08:00:20 - [INFO] - Data Sent Successfully
2026-01-12 08:01:15 - [DATA] - Temperature Sensor Reading: 24.6°C
2026-01-12 08:01:15 - [DATA] - Humidity Sensor Reading: 44.8%
2026-01-12 08:01:18 - [INFO] - Sending Data to Cloud
2026-01-12 08:01:20 - [INFO] - Data Sent Successfully
2026-01-12 08:05:30 - [WARNING] - Temperature Sensor Out of Range: 5.2°C (Min: 10.0°C)
2026-01-12 08:05:32 - [INFO] - Alert Triggered: Under Temperature Detected
2026-01-12 08:05:35 - [INFO] - Sending Alert Notification to User
2026-01-12 08:05:40 - [INFO] - Alert Notification Sent Successfully
2026-01-12 08:10:00 - [INFO] - Device Status Check: All Systems Operational
```

Figure 4.1: RTT log of IoT device

We can see a timestamp, different log levels, and human-readable information.

Such a log already gives us key information about our system. We can immediately check if the log order is as expected. Are the timestamps as expected or not?

So, even with something as simple as a system log, we can already get a better understanding of our running system without having to interact with it directly.

Next, let's look at a more sophisticated approach with code instrumentation. For this, I will be using SystemView. The example projects will run the RTOS embOS. In this case, the RTOS kernel is already instrumented out of the box with the SystemView API, but you can apply the same principles to any target application as long as you have a host application that can interpret and visualize the recorded data.

Our first example will show a simple application with multiple tasks.

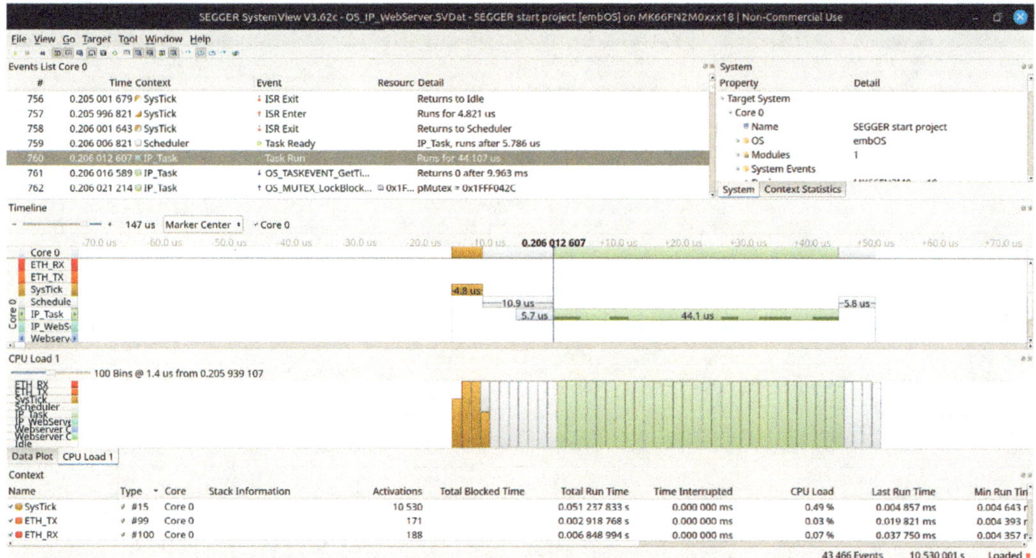

Figure 4.2: SystemView recording of embOS

The underlying principle of this recording is still logging. But as we can see, the result is vastly different from the classic log that we saw in *Figure 4.1*. We can see the task scheduler switching between different RTOS tasks. We can see the exact timing of each task call and the switching time. There is additional information about the system context, such as CPU load and usage statistics for each task and interrupt that we have instrumented in our system.

But we can extract even more information from the system. This next example will run on a triple-core setup, and we will export the data from an accelerometer, which will also be displayed on the same time axis as the system timeline.

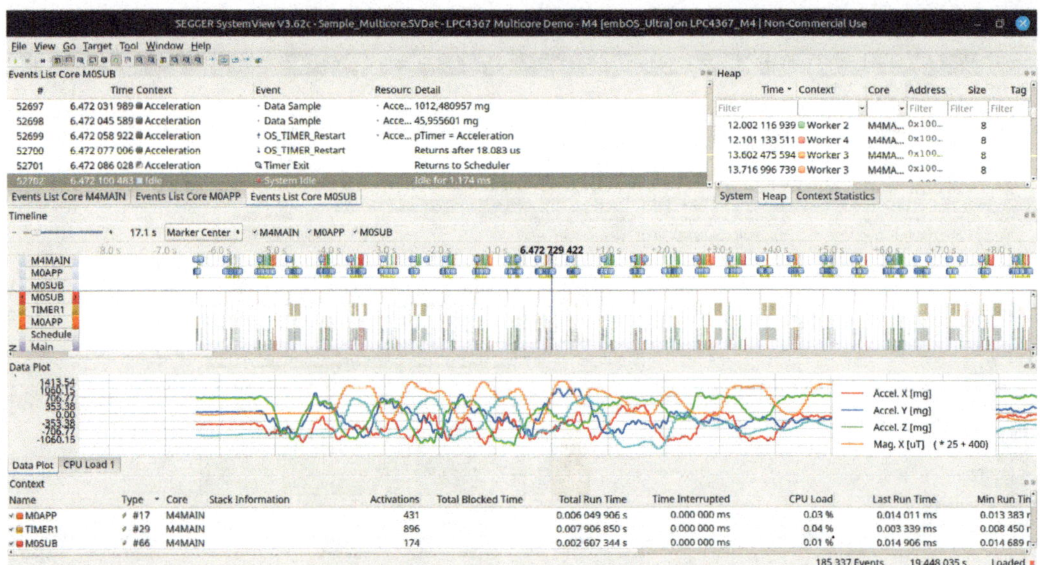

Figure 4.3: SystemView recording of multi-core system with additional data

This time, we have the **Data Plot** window open, which shows us the recorded sensor data referenced to the main timeline, showing us the system tasks and interrupts. Additionally, in the top-right corner, we can see information about heap memory actions of the system, which gives us an even deeper system insight.

From these graphs and tables alone, we can extract a multitude of different information from the target device while it is running without needing any specialized trace equipment, as we are simply using the debug interface to extract the data in this scenario using RTT.

However, while software tracing has clear advantages such as availability and portability, it will always be an intrusive trace technique that is not always viable.

The next section will show an alternative that addresses this problem.

Hardware tracing

In this section, we will learn about hardware tracing, its prerequisites, and how it can be used to deepen your system insight.

What is hardware tracing?

Hardware tracing is a special subtype of tracing where a particular hardware feature is used to extract trace information. In most cases, the data extraction is non-intrusive. That means that it does not have any runtime impact on your target application, and thus, you can verify a system without changing its behavior.

There are several hardware tracing methods, and we will focus on those available for Arm Cortex-M devices.

Which methods are available?

On Arm Cortex-M, we essentially have two hardware trace variants available to us. The key differences are whether the trace method is gapless, how many output interfaces are supported, and what the maximum bandwidth is.

ITM

Let's start with the **Instrumentation Trace Macrocell (ITM)**, which is available on most older Armv7M devices [2]. It is an Arm CoreSight trace unit that is directly connected to the core.

The main features of the ITM are as follows:

- Stimulus ports for logging
- Periodic PC (**program counter**) samples
- Event tracing
- Timestamps on event triggers
- Data tracing

Depending on how it is configured, the ITM will generate packets based on certain actions of the MCU, which can then be collected by a debug probe.

We can already see that an ITM can offer a large range of different features that can give us more information about our target system while it is running.

The most common output interface for the ITM is the SWO pin that was introduced in *Chapters 2* and *3*. Typically SWO would be used as an output interface for `printf` debugging via so called ITM stimulus ports, but it can also be used to collect periodic PC samples to get an execution history of your target device. *Figure 4.4* shows the typical data flow path for the trace data from the core to the SWO pin.

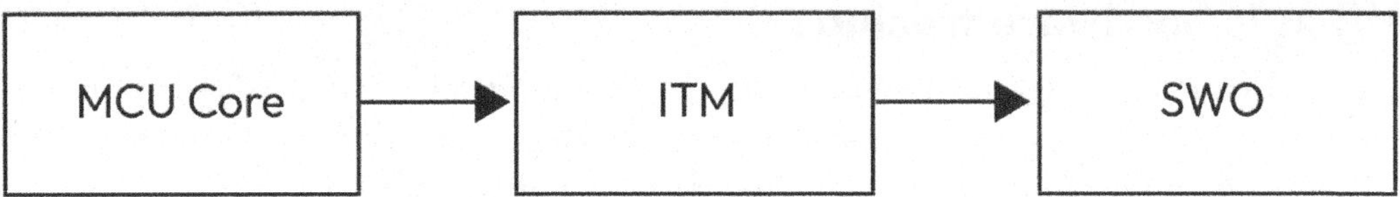

Figure 4.4: Diagram showing ITM data flow

Alternatively, the data can be output via the **Trace Port Interface Unit (TPIU)** [2]. This is the parallel trace port that was introduced in *Chapter 2*, which is specified by Arm to have one clock signal and up to 4 data signals. On modern Armv8M target devices, you will more likely find a TPIU as the output channel via the parallel port instead of SWO. That is mostly due to SWO not being multi-core capable and offering a lower maximum bandwidth.

On multi-core devices, you might see a **System Trace Macrocell (STM)** instead, which is the successor to the ITM. The features are comparable to the ITM, but with a focus on handling multiple trace sources at once.

ETM

The other hardware trace variant that is available to us on Armv7M and Armv8M cores is tracing via the **Embedded Trace Macrocell (ETM)** [3].

The ETM also sits next to the core, but instead of generating trace data just periodically or only on certain events, it will track the complete program's execution and provide a gapless history of all executed instructions.

The main output interface is the TPIU. It is recommended to utilize all four data pins of the parallel port to avoid overflows of the interface, as the data rates of the ETM can easily reach over 100 MB/s. The trace clock speed usually follows the CPU clock by a factor of ½.

So, make sure that the board you are using is capable of handling such high speeds on its GPIOs to avoid signal integrity issues.

While, in theory, the Arm debug and trace infrastructure (Arm Coresight) can handle trace data from multiple cores at once, in practice, the bandwidth of the TPIU parallel port is simply insufficient on Cortex-M. Yes, there are ETM features such as stalling and triggers to trace only specific code areas, but it is quite cumbersome to set up such configurations and obtain a reasonable benefit from them. My recommendation is to trace one core at a time if you are on multi-core Cortex-M targets.

An alternative output sink for ETM data is on-chip buffers such as the **Embedded Trace Buffer (ETB)** or **Embedded Trace FIFO (ETF)**. Typically, these are dedicated RAM areas that are reserved for trace only and have varying sizes, typically in the lower kB area (e.g., 64 kB).

Figure 4.5 shows an example data path of a multicore Cortex-M device with multiple trace sources and trace sinks.

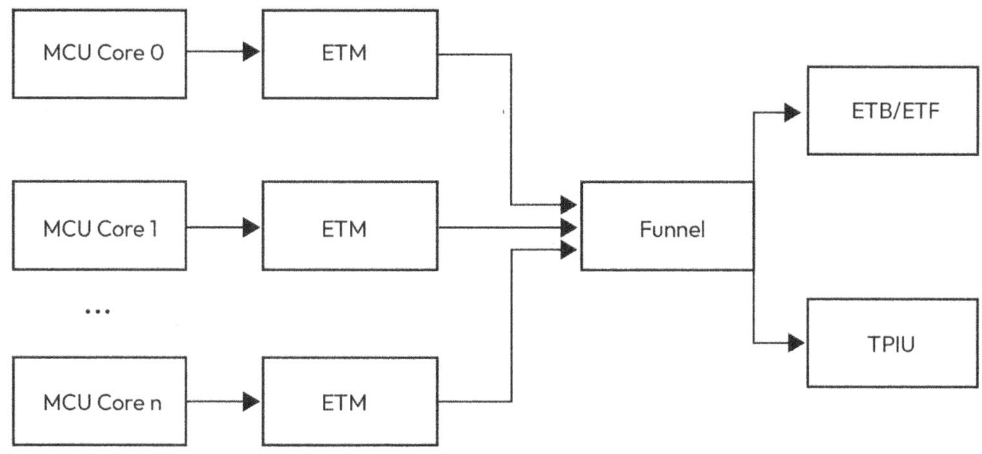

Figure 4.5: Diagram showing data flow for the ETM

The great benefit of a trace buffer is that no additional pins are required, as we can simply use the debug interface to read them out. However, the main drawbacks are that they are not readable while the target device is running and generating trace data. The instruction trace history that can be stored in the buffer is very limited, so only very small recordings are possible, whereas via the parallel port, practically infinite recordings are possible. In this case, the limiting factor is the storage space of your host PC that is connected to the trace probe.

Practical approach

To get started with hardware tracing, we first must check if it is supported by the chip we are looking to trace on. For tracing via the ITM, you will need at least the SWO pin or a TPIU with at least two pins (one clock and one data). Then you will need a debug or trace probe that supports that trace feature.

Finally, it is possible that target-specific initialization steps are required to initialize the pin interface.

The initialization process can usually be split into two stages. First, the **Arm CoreSight** initialization, which covers anything Arm generic that is described in the corresponding Arm reference manuals. This initialization is usually taken care of automatically by your debug or trace probe. The second initialization part is the pin interface itself. Typically, that includes GPIO and clock initialization.

On some older Cortex-M devices, the second stage might not be necessary as fixed addresses were used, and only one set of GPIO pins was trace capable. When in doubt, consult your device's reference manual. Modern Cortex-M devices nearly always require some sort of target-specific initialization steps.

For ETM-tracing, the story is quite similar. We have two initialization stages: one is, again, the CoreSight initialization, and the other is the chip-specific one.

Other than the ETM and TPIU, there is also an optional component called the **trace funnel**, which also requires configuration. It is usually available on devices that have multiple trace sources (e.g., due to having multiple cores).

Luckily, Arm specifies something called a ROM table, which is a neat feature specifically useful for probe vendors, as it contains crucial information about the core's debug logic and available features, which can be auto-detected by the debug or trace probe.

That way, under ideal conditions, the Arm-specific CoreSight initialization can be done automatically, as the debug probe can autodetect all required information from the ROM table.

The device-specific initialization usually involves initializing the trace pins for the TPIU and setting up the trace clock. Most trace probes on the market offer some sort of script interface to which this initialization can be offloaded. I recommend using these script interfaces, even though it is possible in most cases to perform the initialization from your target application as well.

The main drawbacks of doing the initialization from your target application are that you will not be able to trace from the beginning of the application, and you risk leaving potential debug code in your release application, which is usually something to be avoided.

Many probe vendors will try to make the trace features as easy to use as possible and might even have example configurations or scripts available to get started quickly. So, simply keep an eye out for this when shopping for a new trace probe.

Okay, now that we have learned what needs to be done to enable the feature, how can we use it to our advantage?

The main benefits of hardware tracing and, more specifically, instruction tracing, are that we gain access to the following debug and analysis features:

- Analyzing full application backtrace
- Code coverage
- Code profiling

Let's get into the details of these features one by one.

Backtrace recording

By being able to record the program flow, we can later reconstruct the application's execution path exactly and verify if the application was behaving as expected. Combined with debug symbols, we can reference the recorded PC addresses to source lines and create, essentially, a time machine for our code.

While this data can be recorded by both ITM and ETM, the quality of the ETM data is vastly superior, as we have a gapless recording, whereas ITM data will only be periodic or event-driven.

Figure 4.6 shows an example ETM backtrace recording in Ozone.

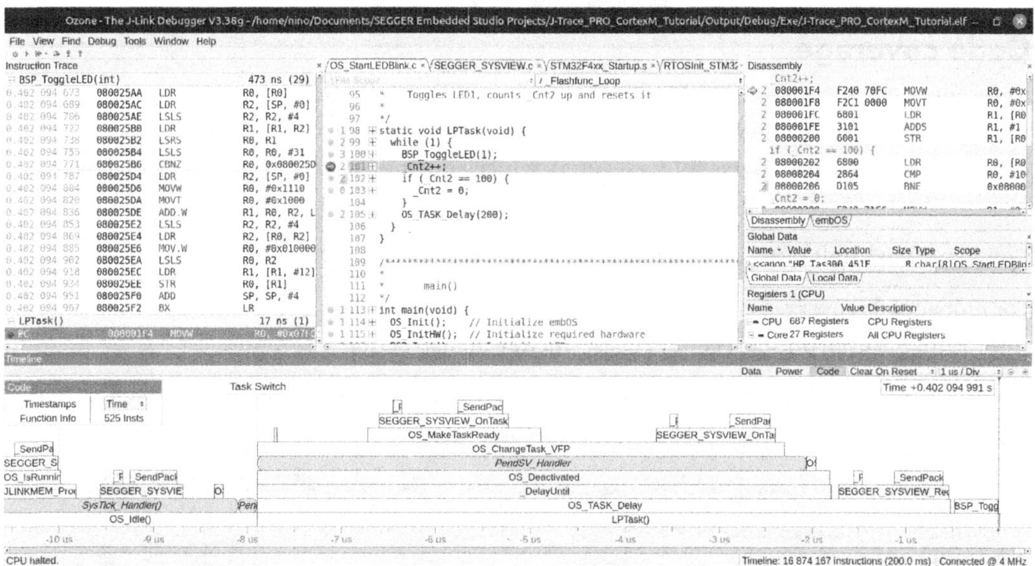

Figure 4.6: Backtrace recording in Ozone

In the **Instruction Trace** window, we can see the recorded trace data and each instruction that was executed. The latest executed instructions are at the bottom of the list. Additionally, Ozone not only references the backtrace data with the source code, but it also draws a so-called flame graph in the **Timeline** window, giving us a visual reference.

Video 4.1 shows how we can step back through the application and see how we ended up at the current halted state of the system.

To access the videos in this chapter, go to `https://packt.link/Zzn1s`, or scan the following QR code:

Code coverage

Code coverage is the measure of how much of your code has actually been fully executed. It is very useful for testing and verifying your code. By gathering instruction traces, we can measure exactly which code parts were fully executed, which code paths were taken, and which were not.

Combined with unit tests, this method can be very useful.

For proper code coverage analysis, I recommend using the gapless ETM data so you can apply this technique even on short code ranges, since each instruction is recorded.

Figure 4.7 shows an example code coverage output of a simple `if` clause that will evaluate to `true` if the counter variable `_Cnt2` reaches the value `100`:

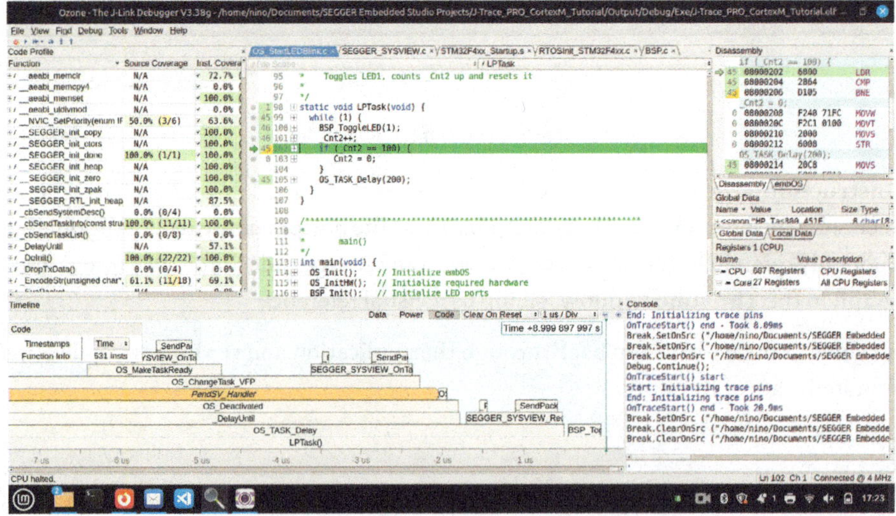

Figure 4.7: Code coverage before if clause fully covered

As we can see, next to the code lines on the left are color blocks that are white, green, or orange.

White means that this line has not been executed at all yet. Green means that the line was fully executed, and orange means that this code line was partially executed. In this case, *line 102* is marked partially green and partially orange. The reason is that the if clause was evaluated at least once, and thus all instructions that are matched with this code line have been fetched by the MCU but not yet fully executed. For non-conditional instructions, fully executed means executed at least once. For conditional instructions, fully executed means that the instruction must be executed once and not executed once by not matching the instruction's condition requirements. So, for full coverage of a conditional instruction, it must be fetched at least twice.

In this case, we can see in the **Disassembly** window which instruction was not fully executed yet. It is the BNE instruction. To avoid diving too deeply into the Arm instruction set, I will briefly explain what this instruction does. It is short for **Branch if Not Equal**, meaning that the instruction branches to the destination address each time the value comparison from before does not evaluate to true. That is the case for all fetches of this instruction so far, as long as the variable does not reach the value 100. The moment it does reach 100, the BNE instruction will be fetched but not executed and thus be marked as fully executed, which we can see in *Figure 4.8*:

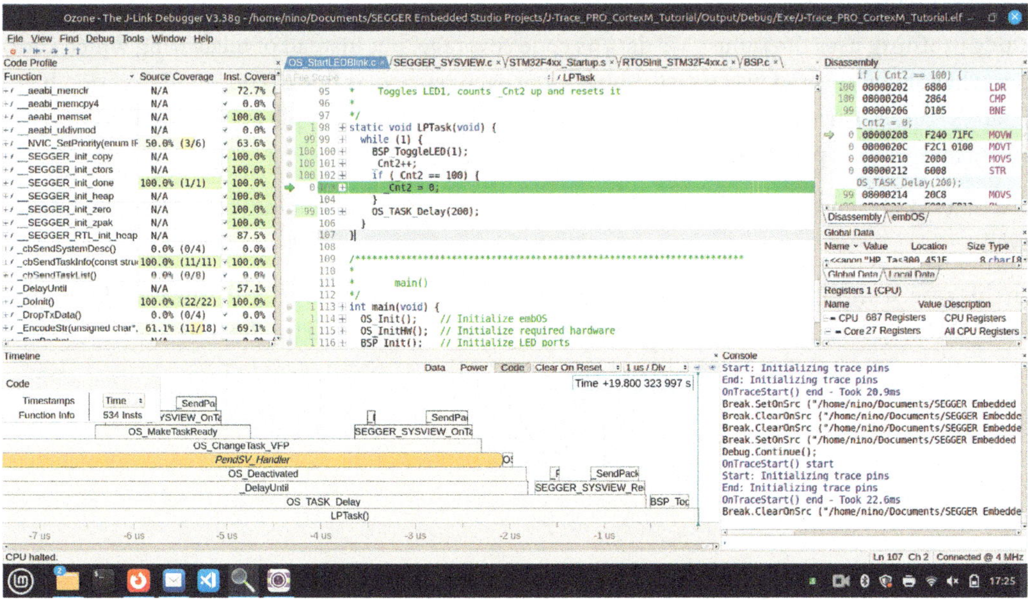

Figure 4.8: Code coverage after if clause is fully covered

There are several different coverage types that can result in different qualities of coverage reports.

The main types are as follows:

- **Function coverage**: Checks if every function or subroutine has been called
- **Statement coverage**: Checks which statements in the program have been executed
- **Branch coverage**: Checks which program junctions (branch points) have been executed
- **Condition coverage**: Checks if each Boolean sub-expression has evaluated both false and true
- **Modified condition/decision coverage (MC/DC)**: Checks if every entry and exit point of a method has been invoked at least once, and if every decision took every possible outcome
- **Parameter value coverage (PVC)**: Checks if all input variants of a method are covered

The first four coverage methods can usually be done with hardware tracing directly. The last two require additional mutations of your application and, in some cases, specifically built test cases to prove that type of coverage, so it is not always available out of the box.

Code profiling

Code profiling uses the same base data as code coverage, but instead of measuring which code parts have been covered, we measure how often each particular line of code or instruction has been executed. This can be very useful when trying to determine application hotspots to further improve application performance or efficiency.

If a timestamp source is available, we can also measure the execution time for different calls as well.

In this case, using an ITM is also viable, since over long runtimes, we can do statistical hot spot analysis, which can still provide great insight into your system. But for the best trace experience, ETM is definitely the better choice.

Figure 4.9 shows an example of a code profiling result:

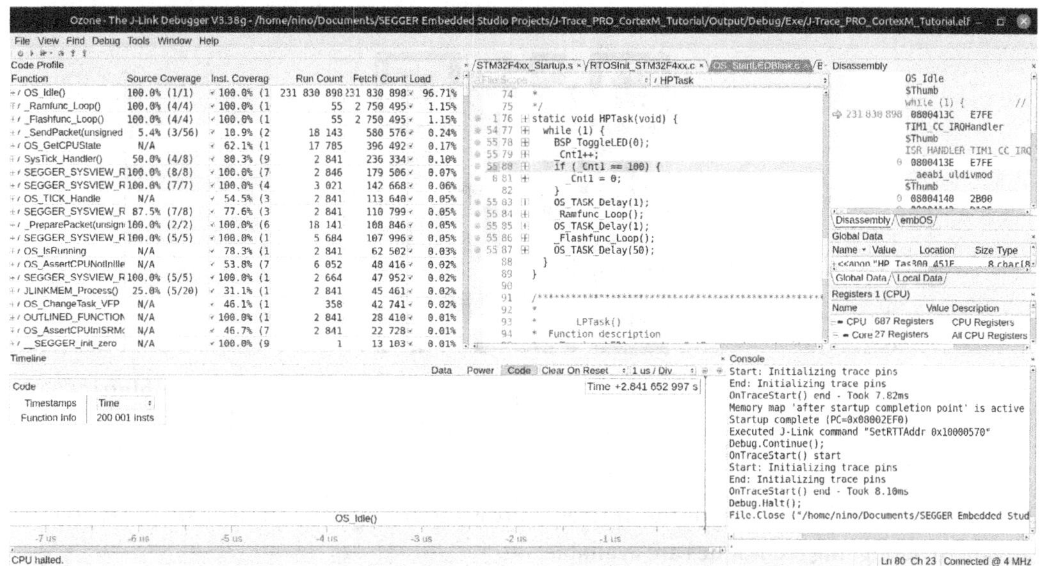

Figure 4.9: Code profiling result

In the preceding screenshot, we can see various counters in the **Code Profile** window, but also in the source lines themselves. From the run and fetch counters, Ozone also calculates the total CPU load of each function so we can do a hot-spot analysis on the fly. In this example, we can see that the application spends roughly 96% of the CPU time in OS_Idle(). Since this is just a simple blinky example, this is expected behavior, but if that function were something that was expected to execute only briefly and not waste many CPU cycles, it would be a main target for code optimization.

And best of all, code profiling can even be done completely non-intrusively while the target is running. This is showcased in *Video 4.2*.

To access the videos in this chapter, go to `https://packt.link/Zzn1s`, or scan the following QR code:

All in all, hardware tracing is a very powerful tool that can tip the scales when running into unexpected issues, whether for fixing hard-to-track-down bugs or complementing our automated unit tests with real hardware tests.

Now that we have learned about the different hardware tracing variants, let's see what other advanced debugging techniques are available.

Live symbol tracking

This section will dive deeper into the topic of live symbol tracking and explain how it can be utilized and which variants are available on Arm Cortex-M.

What is live symbol tracking?

Live symbol tracking is the process of tracking variable values while the target device is running. We can either track the global variables that we can extract from the debug symbols, or we can track specific memory locations or memory-mapped peripherals.

Next, we will learn which sampling methods are available.

RTT

Let's start with the most obvious choice, `printf` via RTT. We simply periodically store the variable value in the RTT buffer and let the debug probe grab it whenever possible.

This has the great benefit that we can do synchronous variable tracking, as we determine the exact moment when the variable is read and stored. The main drawback, just as before, is that this process is intrusive and requires some system memory.

Background memory access

In *Chapter 3*, we learned that on Cortex-M devices, we can manipulate various memory types while the target is halted. But what I did not tell you was that we can do so while the target device is running as well.

This is done via an Arm feature called **background memory access**. It allows us to use the data bus with our debug probe at the same time as the MCU.

That way, we can non-intrusively sample variable values. The sampling rate depends on the capabilities of the debug probe and the maximum debug interface speed of the chip, as we are simply utilizing the standard debug interface without needing extra pins.

Keep in mind that this type of live symbol tracking is asynchronous, as the variable is only sampled whenever the debug probe is able to do so, which is not guaranteed to be at equal time intervals.

Data tracing via ITM

The ITM can also be used to track variable values via the stimulus ports. But just like RTT, this approach is intrusive. Additionally, we have to use at least one additional pin if we send the data via the SWO pin. The benefit of the ITM in comparison to RTT is that it does not use system memory for the data transfer.

Data tracing via ETM

Technically, ETM tracing also specifies data tracing. However, it is implementation-defined whether it is available or not, and you will only very rarely see it implemented on Cortex-M targets, simply because the bandwidth of the trace port is very limited on Cortex-M, and data tracing can become very bandwidth-hungry pretty quickly. But at least the live tracking of symbols would be non-intrusive, so it might be worth the effort depending on the debug scenario.

Practical approach

This time, we will focus on the most straightforward strategy of the four methods, which is live symbol tracking via background memory access.

As we are using a J-Link debug probe, the feature is called **High-Speed Sampling (HSS)**.

It can simply be enabled in Ozone by either watching a specific variable or memory address and enabling the periodic refresh of that symbol.

Watched Data 1						
Expression	Value	Location	Size	Refresh	Type	Scope
_Cnt1	45	1000 0800	4	5 Hz	int	OS_StartLEDBlink.c
_Cnt2	12	1000 07FC	4	5 Hz	int	OS_StartLEDBlink.c

Figure 4.10: Live variable watch in Ozone

Or, you can add symbols to the data sampling window, where you can select different sampling rates, usually in the kHz range.

Data Sampling								Sampling Freq: 10 kHz
Expression	Type	Value	Min	Max	Average	# Changes	Min. Change	Max. C
_Cnt1	int	62	0	62	31.2388115	62	0	1
_Cnt2	int	16	0	16	8.49139309	16	0	1

Figure 4.11: Data Sampling window in Ozone

The data can then either be exported to a file for external editing or plotted into a graph as shown in *Video 4.3*.

To access the videos in this chapter, go to `https://packt.link/Zzn1s`, or scan the following QR code:

Live data sampling is an excellent tool to visualize, for example, sensor data or input values for dynamic circuits such as motor control.

Now that we have learned how to live with sample variables, let's see how the same can be done for the power usage of the system.

Power profiling

In this section, we will learn about power profiling, how it can be used for system analysis, and which methods are available.

What is power profiling?

Power profiling describes a method of measuring the electrical power consumption of a target system over time. Typically, the physical unit that is being recorded is the electric current. The reason is simply that the voltage is usually fixed on embedded systems, so the variance in power delivery that we are looking for will be most pronounced in the current consumption of a system.

That way, we can detect power consumption patterns and optimize for power efficiency. On embedded systems, it is crucial to use a power profiling method that offers very high resolution, at least in the µA range, and a sampling rate that is high enough to capture even fast switching sequences, which are very common in embedded applications. Sampling rates at least in the high kHz range are recommended.

While the most common approach is to measure the power consumption of the total system, it is also possible to split your system into smaller, separate power domains and focus the measurements on only certain components in your system (e.g., only the MCU, only sensors, only memory, etc.).

That way, you have full flexibility in choosing which system component you want to optimize, as sometimes, in a full system analysis, high current draw components may drown out the other components that you want to analyze.

Which methods are available?

There are two main methods to acquire power profiling measurements, and both require some consideration in your hardware design.

The first is measuring via a shunt resistor. Here, a very low-ohmage resistor of a known value is placed in series with the target supply connection. On both sides of the shunt, there are typically measurement points.

To get the current consumption, we now simply use an accurate voltage measurement system that connects to the two measurement points. That way, we can measure the voltage drop across the shunt resistor.

With good old Ohm's Law, $U = R*I$, where U is the voltage, R is the resistance, and I is the current, we can then calculate the current passing through the resistor by rearranging the equation to $I = U/R$ [4].

However, this approach has a few drawbacks.

- The approach is intrusive as the measurement itself will alter the power consumption of the system
- Resistor variability may produce non-comparable results between different boards
- Circuit modification may be required
- Measurement range is limited by the shunt resistor rating

The other, less common method is to use a tool that provides power delivery to the system itself and has built-in current measurement capabilities. If combined with the power delivery pins that the debug interface offers, as introduced in *Chapter 2*, we can even build debug probes with that feature.

This approach removes some of the shunt resistor drawbacks, as the measurement setup can be calibrated in the factory, so the measurement itself does not alter the outcome. However, this approach also requires some circuit modification, although it is much more easily planned in, as you will need some form of power delivery circuit anyway, and designing a lane that goes to the debug port is usually not an issue.

Both are viable methods, which in the end will provide you with similar results, assuming both setups are using comparable tooling and specifications.

Practical approach

In the following example, I will be using the second method and provide power to my target system via the debug interface using a J-Trace Pro probe. The probe has a built-in current measurement circuit, and the recorded values can then be easily plotted with Ozone.

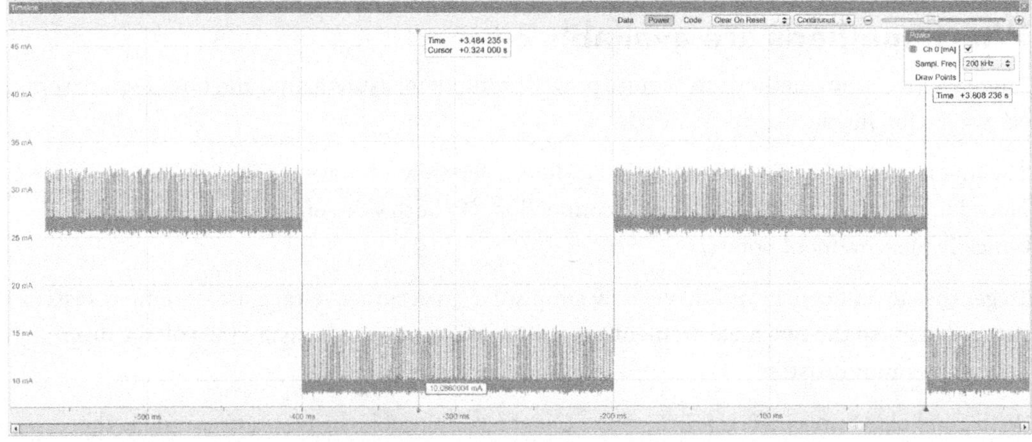

Figure 4.12: Power profiling recording in Ozone

Just like before, with live data sampling, we get periodic measurement results from the probe, which can either be exported or plotted into a timeline. This can be used alongside other debug techniques to directly see the application's impact on power consumption when running certain code parts. One such feature can be hardware tracing. If we correlate these two information sources in the same timeline view, we can visualize how the code has impacted the current draw of the system.

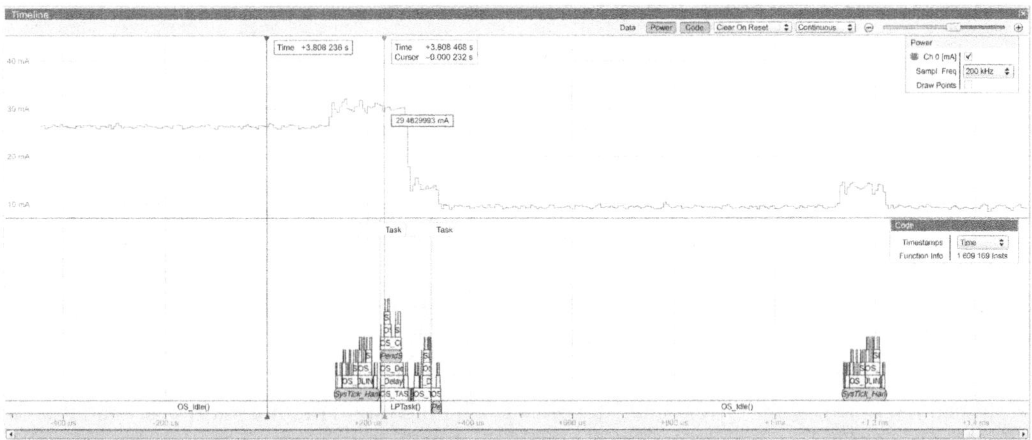

Figure 4.13: Power profiling recording merged with instruction trace data

In *Figure 4.12*, we can see the result of two LEDs being switched on and off at different times, which gives us this distinctive pattern. The little bumps we see are not clear from the power recording alone, but adding the context of instruction tracing to the recording makes them clearer.

In *Figure 4.13*, we can see the correlation with the executed code and can indeed verify that the task that handles LED toggling is triggered when the power drop happens. On the power bumps, we can see that a `SysTick_Handler` interrupt executes. So, we can even see when certain chip features are activated.

While it is possible to gain system insight with just the power measurement, it becomes much more valuable when combining it with some event log or timestamps from the target device that can correlate the recorded current measurement with the actual executed code. So, keep an eye out for this combination when shopping for power profiling capable tools.

Now that we have learned how to measure the power consumption of our system while it is executing code, let's next look at RTOS-based multi-tasking setups.

RTOS awareness

In this section, we will talk about RTOS debugging, how it is different from a bare-metal application, and what information is required by a debugger to correctly recreate RTOS task states.

What is RTOS awareness?

First, we must understand what is different between a bare-metal application and an RTOS. **Bare-metal applications** usually run inside an infinite loop. All application methods (except interrupts), modules, state machines, and so on are called from that main infinite loop routine and have to be handled manually.

This is simple, small, and fast. But this approach does not scale well and becomes hard to maintain as the application becomes more complex.

This is where RTOS-based applications shine. Each application method or module is enclosed in its own task with its own context and stack. The scheduling of each task is handled automatically, thus making it an excellent basis for multitasking applications whose scope may become more complex over time. The price is a bit of system memory and overhead due to task scheduling.

But what does that mean for a debugger? A bare-metal application is straightforward. Any time you halt your application, you see the exact global system state that is valid for all application parts at that point in time. Without extra information, a debugger will assume that this is always the case for the currently running application.

But as mentioned earlier, in an RTOS, we have a unique system context and state for each task that is active. Each task has its own stack. If you halt the application with your debugger in one task and inspect the stack information, that information will be invalid for another task that might be scheduled to run next. To be able to get the debug and stack information from other tasks that are active, we somehow have to make the debugger aware of the RTOS that is running on the target device.

How can this be achieved?

RTOS awareness is typically achieved via some scripting interface that the debug software provides. The script will contain information about the storage locations of the RTOS where the task stack information is stored, as well as additional debug and global data relevant to the RTOS.

This information can include data about the following:

- Semaphores
- Mailboxes
- Interrupts
- Timers
- Watchdogs
- Queues
- Memory pools
- Task stack

The debugger will then read the disclosed memory locations when the target device is halted and reconstruct all necessary information.

Practical approach

In the following examples, we will debug RTOS applications based on the RTOS embOS. Ozone has the necessary RTOS awareness scripts included, so we can start debugging out of the box.

Figure 4.14 shows the task list and the task information.

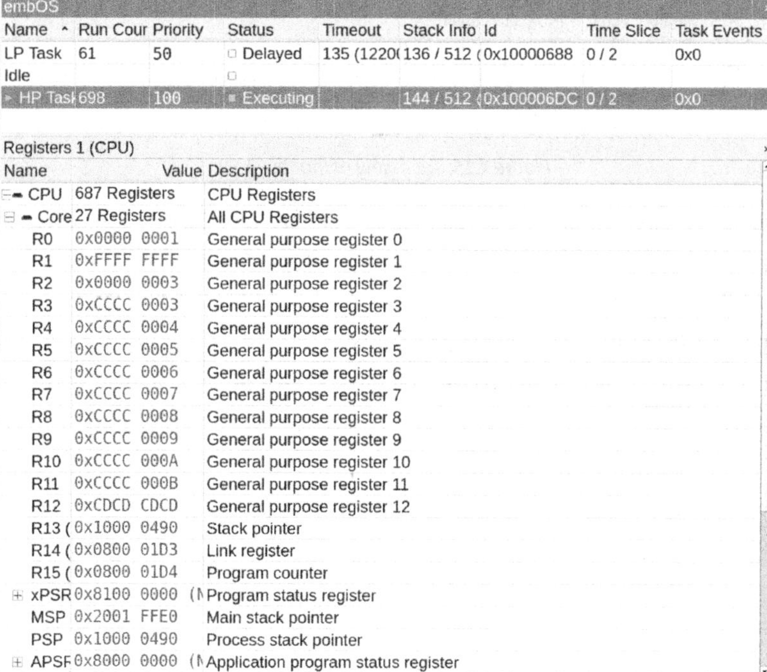

Figure 4.14: Ozone RTOS awareness, task view

As we can see, we are now in the task called `HP Task`. If we double-click on `LP Task` instead, we can see that the CPU registers update accordingly to show the system state the currently highlighted task is in, instead of the task we are actually halted in.

Name	Run Cour	Priority	Status	Timeout	Stack Info	Id	Time Slice	Task Events
▶ LP Task	61	50	■ Delayed	135 (12200)	136 / 512	0x10000688	0 / 2	0x0
Idle			□					
HP Task	698	100	▣ Executing		144 / 512	0x100006DC	0 / 2	0x0

Registers 1 (CPU)

Name	Value	Description
⊟ CPU	687 Registers	CPU Registers
⊟ Core	27 Registers	All CPU Registers
R0	0x1000 0000	General purpose register 0
R1	0xE000 ED04	General purpose register 1
R2	0x0000 0003	General purpose register 2
R3	0x0000 0001	General purpose register 3
R4	0x1000 0000	General purpose register 4
R5	0x0000 0000	General purpose register 5
R6	0xCCCC 0006	General purpose register 6
R7	0xCCCC 0007	General purpose register 7
R8	0xCCCC 0008	General purpose register 8
R9	0xCCCC 0009	General purpose register 9
R10	0xCCCC 000A	General purpose register 10
R11	0xCCCC 000B	General purpose register 11
R12	0xCDCD CDCD	General purpose register 12
R13 (	0x1000 0270	Stack pointer
R14 (	--------	Link register
R15 (	0x0800 0E64	Program counter
⊞ xPSR	0x6100 0000 (r	Program status register
MSP	--------	Main stack pointer
PSP	--------	Process stack pointer
⊞ APSF	--------	Application program status register

Figure 4.15: Task view of inactive task

That way, we can inspect the complete task states even from tasks that are currently not active. The same goes for all other RTOS-related resources that are exposed via the RTOS awareness interface.

If you are doing hardware tracing of an RTOS system, it is even more crucial to have RTOS awareness, otherwise you will get faulty-looking backtrace reconstruction as the debugger is not aware of the scheduler that will reload completely different stack information on each task switch.

In *Figure 4.16*, we can see how it would look if we tried to draw a backtrace timeline without RTOS awareness.

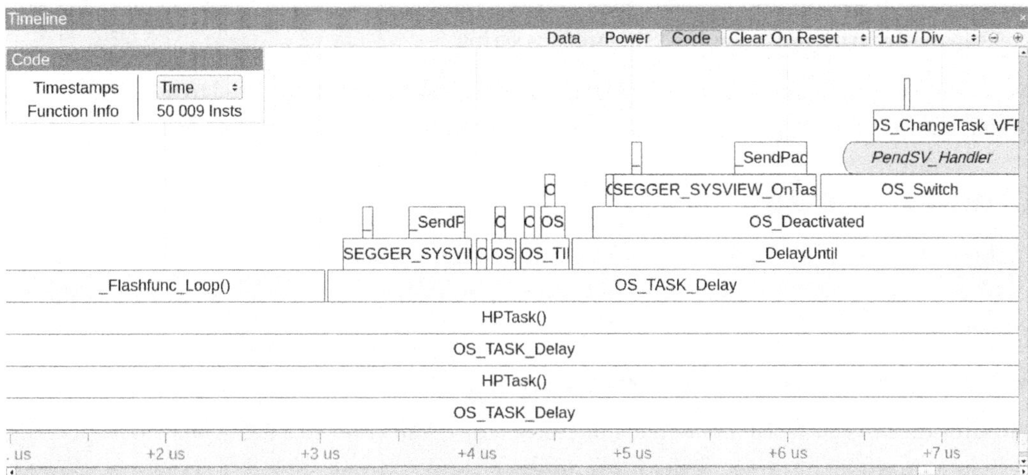

Figure 4.16: RTOS-unaware trace timeline

We see a lot of unexpected stacking and multiple stacked calls of tasks and OS delay functions, which would usually mark the transition between tasks.

Figure 4.17 shows the recording of the same application and how it would look with RTOS awareness enabled.

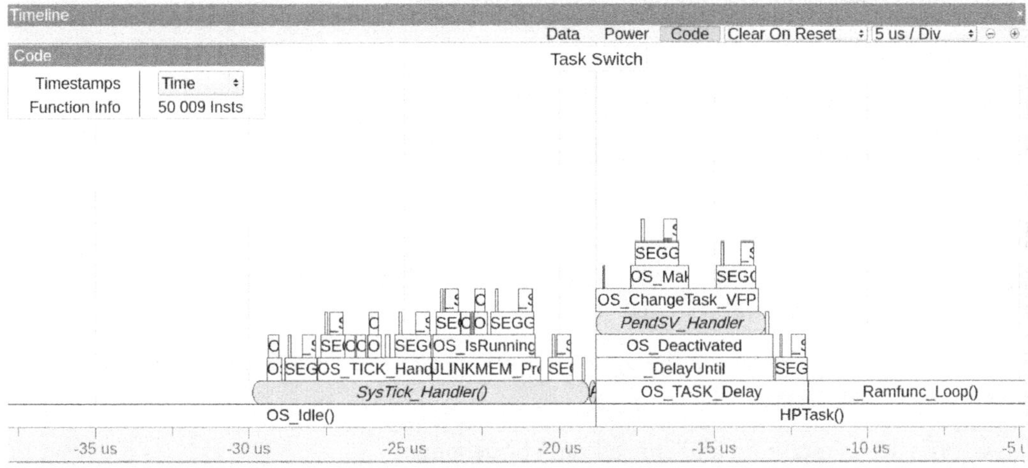

Figure 4.17: RTOS-aware trace timeline

As we can see, having RTOS-aware debugging available to you is crucial, especially when trying to draw a flame graph in the timeline based on instruction trace data. Most debug tool vendors will have the main RTOSs already supported with scripts.

But even if you are using some niche RTOS, most script interfaces are publicly documented, so you can easily write your own RTOS awareness script.

Now that we have learned about RTOS awareness and how it can be utilized to better understand your RTOS system, let's take a look at monitor mode debugging next.

Monitor mode

In this section, we will explore the so-called monitor mode debugging that is available on Arm Cortex-M microcontrollers, and you will learn why and when this is necessary to gain better system insight.

What is monitor mode debugging

Monitor mode is a special mode that a microcontroller can enter so a debugger can inspect the system state while the target device is running.

This is atypical for debugging, as typically you would halt a target device to inspect its system state.

When monitor mode is active on an Arm Cortex-M device and a `halt` command is issued by the debugger, instead of halting the core, the device will enter a special monitor mode interrupt, which will execute the corresponding interrupt handler.

This monitor mode handler must fulfill mainly two tasks:

- Handle debug control commands
- Read/write CPU registers

When can it be applied most efficiently?

Monitor mode is mostly needed in scenarios where you either have communication interfaces that must regularly send keep-alive packets (e.g., Bluetooth) or if you have some external peripheral running that is regulated through the microcontroller and must be updated regularly (e.g., motor control systems).

There are additional limitations and drawbacks that need to be considered when doing monitor mode debugging:

- The debug monitor handler itself can't be debugged
- The monitor mode handler may not alter the stack pointer
- Debugging of higher-priority exceptions than the monitor mode handler is limited
- Device resets must be considered by the application (e.g., a custom `Hardfault` handler) and the debug probe (which needs to restore the monitor mode after reset)

Practical approach

In the following section, we will have monitor mode running on the Cortex-M Trace Reference Board that was introduced in *Chapter 3*. The background task that may not be halted is, for demonstration purposes, a simple LED toggle.

You can find the example project here, in the Git repository:

```
https://github.com/PacktPublishing/-Practical-Debugging-for-Embedded-ARM-
Systems/blob/main/Chapter4/Chapter4_STM32F407_MonitorModeLEDExample_SES.zip
```

The application is straightforward. When the target is running normally, LED0 on the board is blinking. Once the target is halted and control is given to the debug probe, LED1 is blinking instead. This is only possible due to the active debug mode. As mentioned before, this approach can be used in basically any more complex scenario (e.g., Bluetooth communication), where, instead of blinking LED1, you would send keep-alive packets to the connected device so the connection does not break down.

Just like any of the other advanced debug features introduced in this chapter, this feature is invaluable if you have this specific scenario and no other way to debug a certain issue.

Summary

Now that we have made it to the end of this chapter, let's wrap things up.

We have learned about various advanced debug topics, such as software and hardware tracing, variable and power profiling, RTOS awareness, and monitor mode debugging.

Some of these features are unfortunately not always available, so make sure to check beforehand whether your particular target device and your debug setup support these features.

But if they are available, then depending on the situation, they can be invaluable assets when debugging difficult bugs or doing automated testing of your software.

In some industries, it is even mandatory to use advanced analysis features to qualify your software for certification. So, if you are working in such an industry or are planning to do so, it is recommended to hone your skills in that particular feature set.

In the next chapter, we will learn how we can combine different features and methods from *Chapters 3* and *4* to debug certain real-world scenarios.

References

1. Tracing (software): `https://en.wikipedia.org/wiki/Tracing_(software)`

2. CoreSight Component Technical Reference Manual: `https://developer.arm.com/documentation/ddi0314/latest/`

3. Embedded Trace Macrocell Architecture Specification, ETMv4.0 to ETM4.6: `https://developer.arm.com/documentation/ihi0064/latest/`

4. Ohm's law: `https://en.wikipedia.org/wiki/Ohm%27s_law`

Join our community on Discord

Join our community's Discord space for discussions with the authors and other readers: `https://packt.link/embeddedsystems`

5

From Theory to Practice

In this final chapter, we will explore several real-world scenarios that will arise at one point or another in the life of an embedded software engineer. I will show strategies for tackling these issues and demonstrate how the debug techniques and features from *Chapters 3* and *4* can be used and combined to arrive at a quick solution.

In the end, debugging is kind of like solving a puzzle, and you simply have to have the correct mindset when approaching a bug. The tools are just there to make your life easier.

In this chapter, we will cover the following main topics:

- Crash analysis
- Watchdog handling
- Priority pitfalls
- Automated testing
- Memory leaks
- Buffer overflows
- Null pointers
- Communication interfaces

Technical requirements

The following hardware and software components are used in this chapter:

- J-Trace PRO for Cortex-M
- Renesas EK-RA8M1 board with on-board debug probe
- Cortex-M Trace Reference Board (based on ST STM32F407)
- SEGGER Embedded Studio IDE

- Ozone debug software
- SystemView
- Linux Mint 22.2 on host PC

While the hardware components will need to be purchased, the software components can be evaluated and downloaded for free from the software vendor's website.

All of the code in the chapter can be found in the book's GitHub repository: `https://github.com/PacktPublishing/-Practical-Debugging-for-Embedded-ARM-Systems`

Crash analysis

In this first section, we will learn about system crashes and how they can be debugged and analyzed. They are one of the most prominent bug types that you will encounter in your programs, and because they are usually system-breaking bugs, it is crucial to understand and resolve them.

Which crash types are available on ARM Cortex-M?

There are multiple crash types that can occur on an ARM Cortex-M system. For each of these, a specific fault interrupt handler is provided by the system. That way, you can distinguish different faults from one another [1].

The main fault types are as follows:

- **HardFault**: Default type that the other faults can escalate to as well
- **MemManage fault**: Handles memory access violations if a **Memory Protection Unit (MPU)** is used
- **BusFault**: Handles any generic memory access violations
- **UsageFault**: Handles execution errors, for example, division by zero and alignment issues on instruction execution

For each of these fault types, you can find their respective fault handler referenced in the vector table. HardFault is always enabled and has the highest non-configurable priority in the system. If no other fault types are enabled, all faults will raise a HardFault exception.

All other fault types must be enabled specifically via debug control registers. Also, their priorities are configurable, so it is possible to have a peripheral interrupt with a higher priority than a specific fault handler.

Setup information

As an example setup, I will be using the Cortex-M Trace Reference Board and a J-Trace PRO V3 connected to it. You can find the example project that will be used here:

```
https://github.com/PacktPublishing/-Practical-Debugging-for-Embedded-ARM-
Systems/blob/main/Chapter5/Chapter5_CortexM_FaultTest.zip
```

The example project has multiple faulty functions that can be activated by simply uncommenting them in the main() function.

As debug software, Ozone V3.38g will be used. As the IDE, I will be using Embedded Studio V8.26.

The software is running on a Linux Mint host system, but the software I am using is cross-platform compatible, so you can simply use what you are familiar with. How to set up each of these tools is described in detail in the software provider's documentation.

Analysis steps

Let's first open the project in Embedded Studio and comment in the _DivideByZero() function in the main() routine. That way, we can start with a classic cause of faults, division by zero. To make sure only the default HardFault handler is active, we also have to comment out define _USE_DISTINCT_FAULTS.

Now let's start debugging the application in Embedded Studio and see what happens.

Make sure that the breakpoints are enabled for vector catches, so the application actually halts when a fault is triggered. Otherwise, the application will simply run the fault handler. By default, most debuggers will have vector catches enabled.

If we let the application run, it will crash and end up at the HardFault handler routine. Great, now what?

Let's look at the information available to us. The first look should go to the call stack window to see whether we can figure out where we came from.

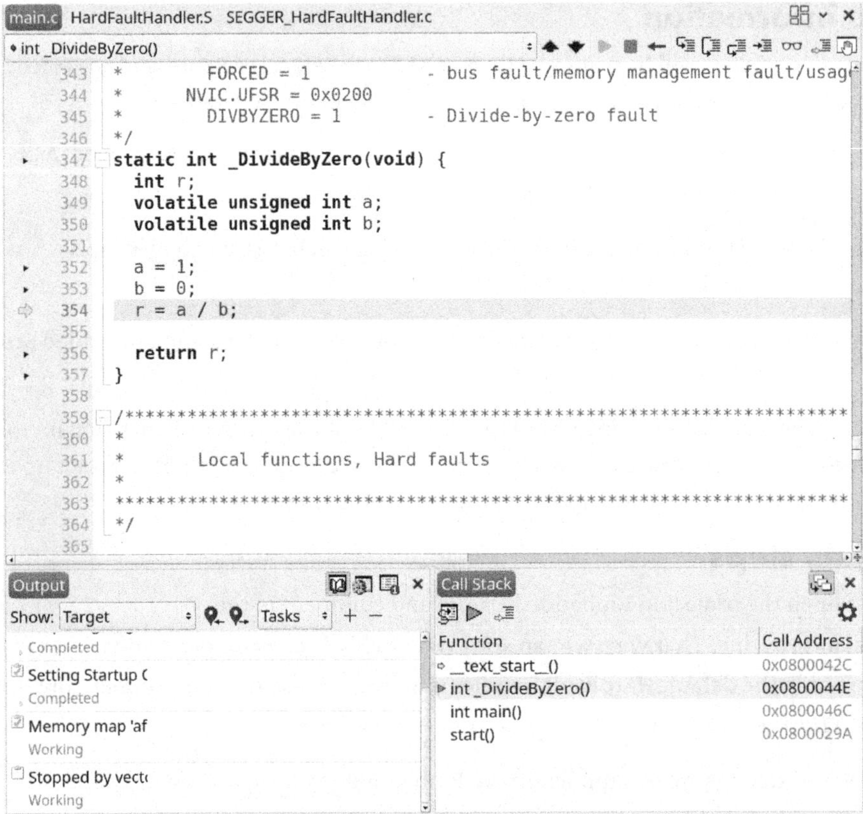

Figure 5.1: Call stack after zero division

In the call stack we see the function call tree that led to the fault. Knowing that the function was called from main() we can assume that the call stack looks intact, so we can see exactly which functions have been called before the fault happened. If we *double-click* on one of the prior functions, the debugger will show us the source code of the function and the exact line where the fault was triggered. Excellent, now we know the area where the fault happened.

Next, we have to understand the context of the function and check what could have caused the fault. We see that there is a calculation happening with multiple variables, and according to the call stack, the crash entry happened on the division of two variables. Let's check the variable values. We can do that either in the respective variable windows (in this case, the **Locals** window), in the watch window, or in some debuggers; we can even hover over the value of the variable, and the value will show up in the tooltip.

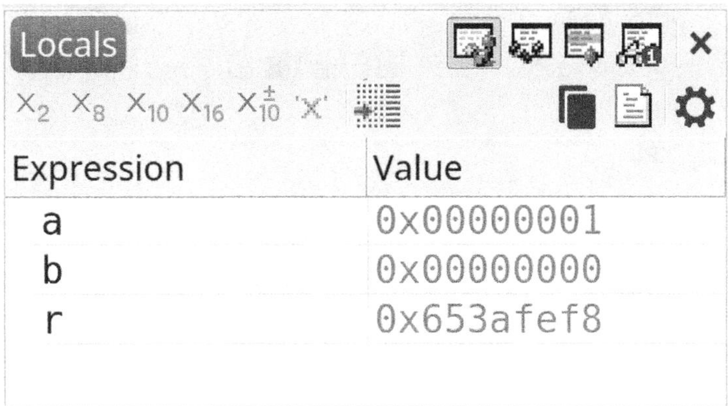

Figure 5.2: Locals window

We can see that variable b had the value 0, and we all know from school that division by zero is illegal, and thus the crash happens on the MCU. This is, of course, a very simplified example, and there will be instances where the analysis is not as straightforward or the expression that is evaluated in the program is more complex, but it shows the general approach to faults. There is no single correct way to do it, but there are more and less reasonable approaches to achieve your goal more quickly, which is finding and fixing the bug.

But this is not all a debugger can tell us about a fault. First, we can uncomment define `_USE_DISTINCT_FAULTS` again and rebuild the application. If we run the application now and run into the fault, we will end up in the UsageFault handler instead of the HardFault handler, which gives us additional information about what fault type we are dealing with, which again can help with analysis. Now we know, for example, that we are not looking for a BusFault.

On ARM Cortex-M microcontrollers, we also have access to the **System Control Block (SCB)**, which is a set of control and status registers that store additional details about the system state, including details about the different fault types.

If we enable the SCB peripheral in Embedded Studio in the **Register** view, we can see the following:

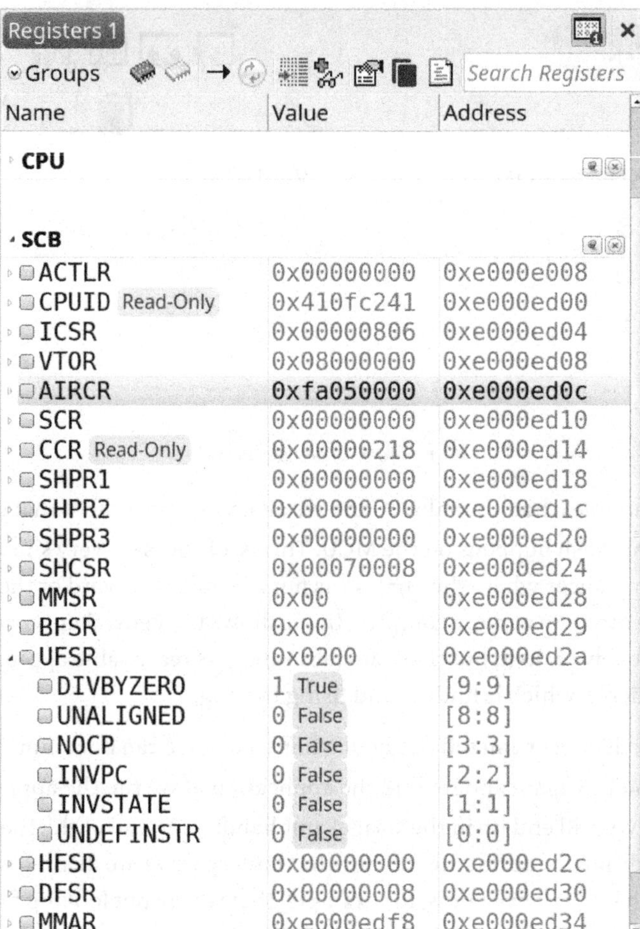

Figure 5.3: SCB Register view

Here, we can see now that in the UFSR register group, which shows additional details for user faults, the value DIVBYZERO is set to 1, which indicates that a division by zero has occurred.

This again gives us additional clues for our analysis of the bug.

On more advanced debuggers such as Ozone, we even get all this extra information presented in a practical extra window, so we can directly understand what the fault type was. In the current fault scenario, the Ozone exception window looks like this:

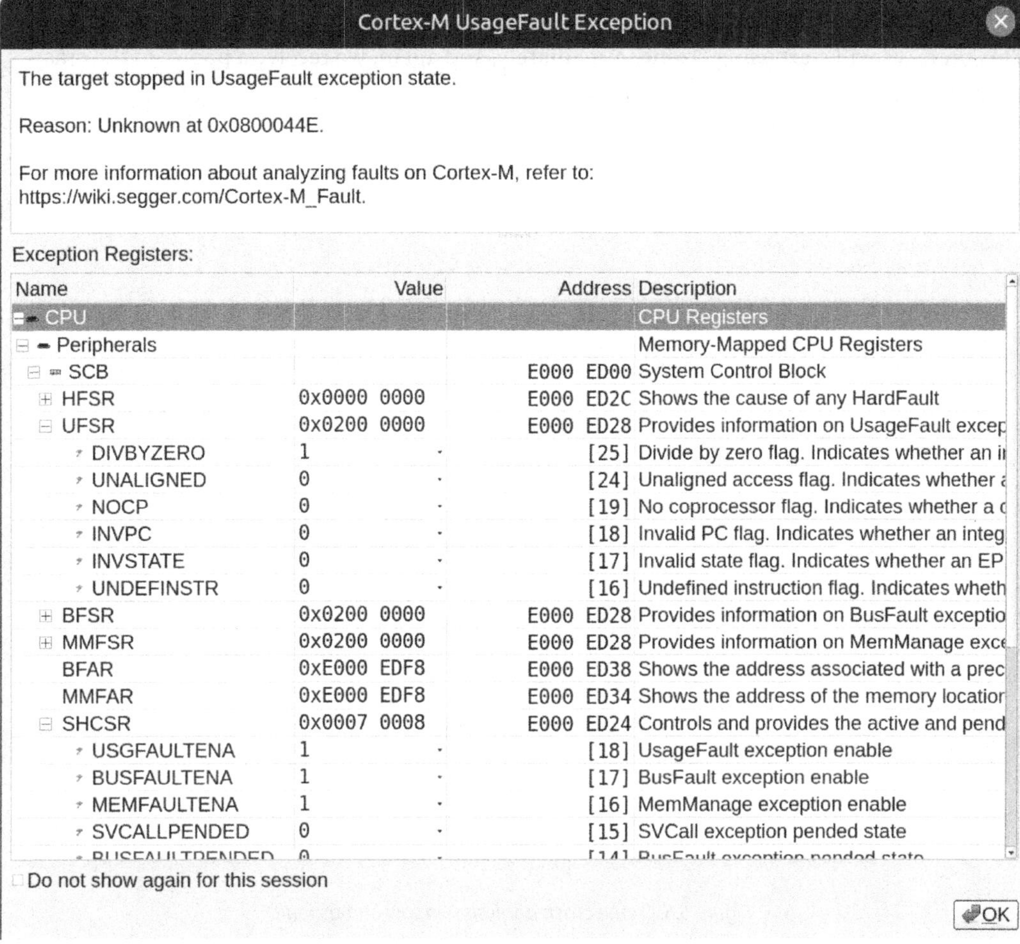

Name	Value	Address	Description
CPU			CPU Registers
Peripherals			Memory-Mapped CPU Registers
SCB		E000 ED00	System Control Block
HFSR	0x0000 0000	E000 ED2C	Shows the cause of any HardFault
UFSR	0x0200 0000	E000 ED28	Provides information on UsageFault excep
DIVBYZERO	1	[25]	Divide by zero flag. Indicates whether an i
UNALIGNED	0	[24]	Unaligned access flag. Indicates whether a
NOCP	0	[19]	No coprocessor flag. Indicates whether a c
INVPC	0	[18]	Invalid PC flag. Indicates whether an integ
INVSTATE	0	[17]	Invalid state flag. Indicates whether an EP
UNDEFINSTR	0	[16]	Undefined instruction flag. Indicates wheth
BFSR	0x0200 0000	E000 ED28	Provides information on BusFault exceptio
MMFSR	0x0200 0000	E000 ED28	Provides information on MemManage exce
BFAR	0xE000 EDF8	E000 ED38	Shows the address associated with a prec
MMFAR	0xE000 EDF8	E000 ED34	Shows the address of the memory location
SHCSR	0x0007 0008	E000 ED24	Controls and provides the active and pend
USGFAULTENA	1	[18]	UsageFault exception enable
BUSFAULTENA	1	[17]	BusFault exception enable
MEMFAULTENA	1	[16]	MemManage exception enable
SVCALLPENDED	0	[15]	SVCall exception pended state
BUSFAULTPENDED	0	[14]	BusFault exception pended state

Figure 5.4: Ozone crash analysis window on usage fault

As we can see, all the SCB register information, and some other details, such as the current address where the fault happened, are neatly displayed in a single view, so you save precious time compared to gathering all this information manually.

Now let's look at another typical fault type: memory access violations.

For this, we have to alter the application again. We comment out `_DivideByZero()` and uncomment `_IllegalWrite()`.

The example scenario is simple: we have a pointer that points to reserved or illegal memory. Then, we try to write a value to the memory location pointed to by that pointer. This obviously fails, and we are greeted with a bus fault.

Now, how can we debug this?

This time, we will start using Ozone immediately, and again, we receive a popup of the crash analysis window.

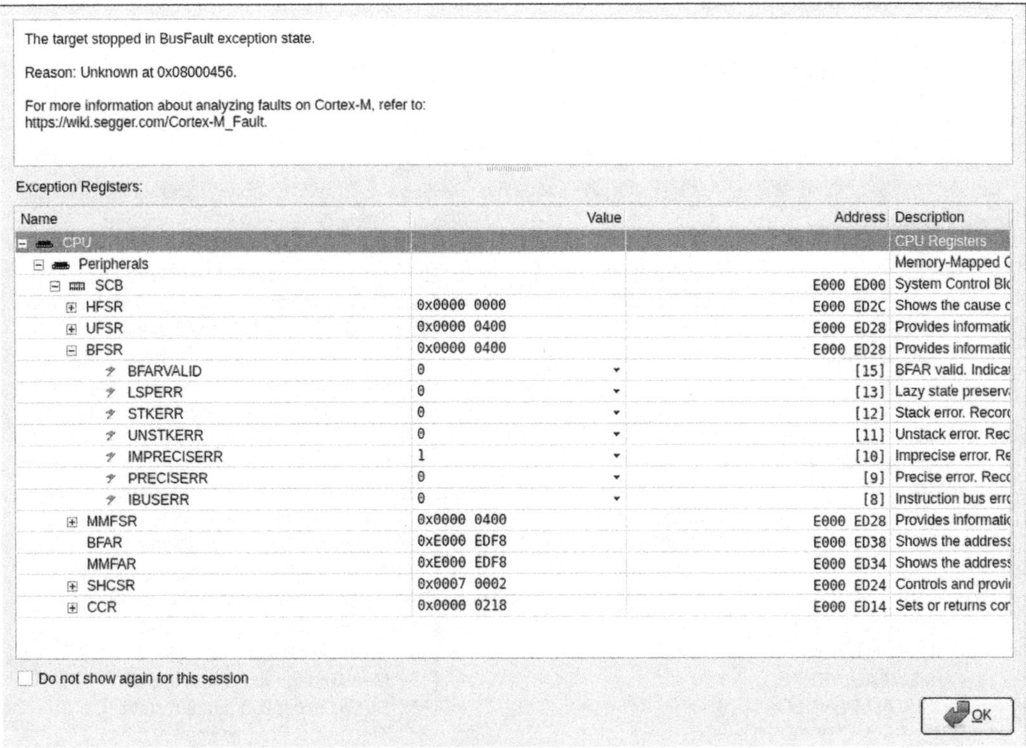

Figure 5.5: Ozone crash analysis window on bus fault

As we can see, the BFSR fields have changed, and the `IMPRECISERR` bit is set. This means that the bus fault that was triggered was imprecise, so the exception was not triggered by exactly the last executed instruction. This makes finding the actual cause of the error a bit more difficult, as we now must potentially investigate multiple instructions before the crash.

This imprecision comes from the fact that memory bus accesses can be asynchronous to the execution pipeline. So, if a store instruction is issued to save a value to a memory address, the write command is sent out to the bus; however, the CPU does not wait for the result of the store operation and instead already loads up the next instructions. Due to that, multiple clock cycles can pass between an illegal read/write operation and the point in time when the exception is actually triggered by the memory bus logic and propagated to the CPU.

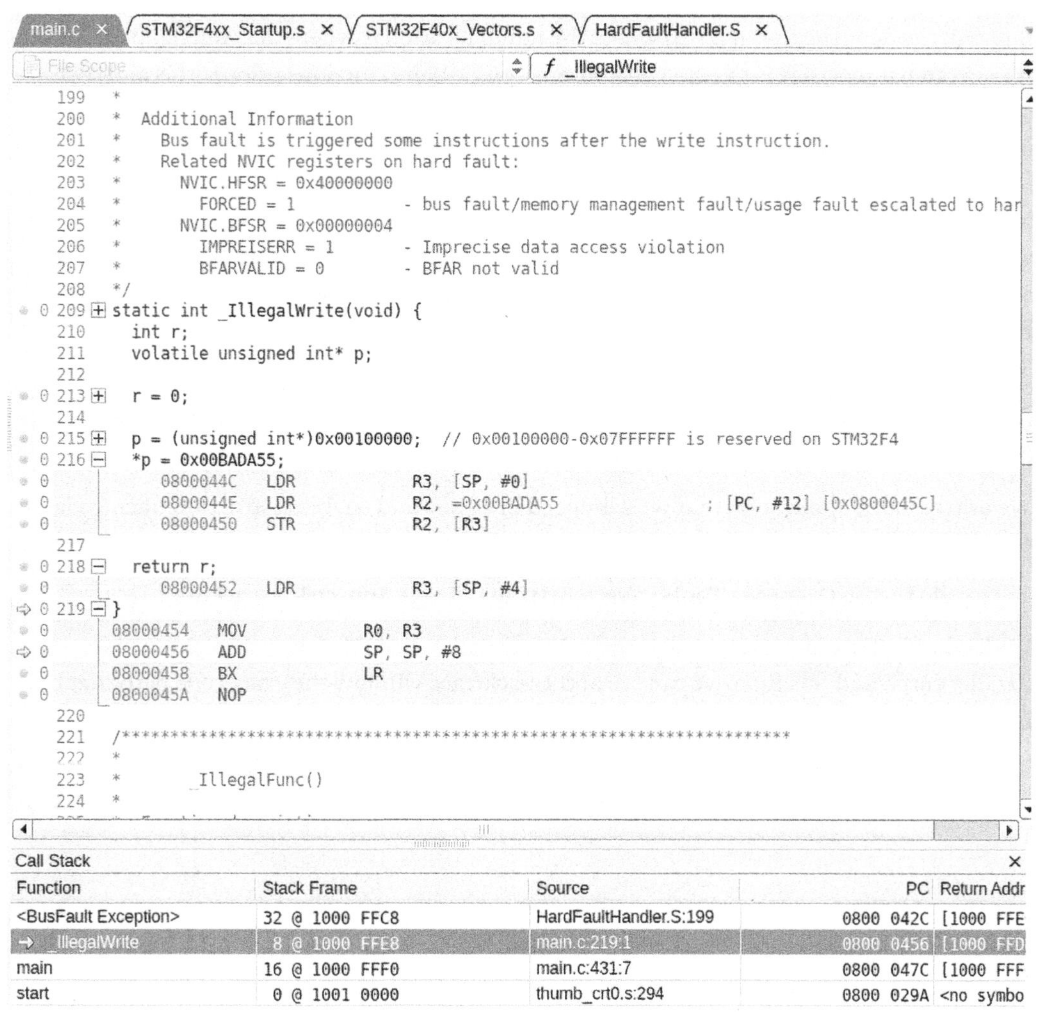

Figure 5.6: Ozone call stack on BusFault

According to the call stack, the exception triggered when the CPU was executing address `0x08000456`, which is an ADD instruction. However, we can see in the inline disassembly that the ADD instruction is not altering the memory whatsoever and thus could not have caused the crash. As this is a very simple example, we can see that the actual culprit must be the STR instruction a couple of lines earlier, but this nicely demonstrates how multiple instructions can pass in some cases before such a fault is triggered.

But with the debugger, we learned where the rough location is where the fault happens, so one way to catch it precisely is to set a breakpoint a couple of instructions prior to this and then step over the instructions to see which one will fail. Stepping is slow enough for even an imprecise bus fault to trigger immediately, so we can find out that way where exactly the crash happened. All that remains is to find out why it crashed by investigating the addresses that are accessed and verifying with, for example, the device's reference manual, whether we are still in valid memory space or not. If not, we would further try to find out what part of the code has altered our pointer in a way that would cause this crash. The memory access fault could also have been triggered in another function that was called before this function.

As a follow up scenario, let's assume we have severe system fault where we do not even have a clean call stack anymore, so we can't determine how we ended up in the fault handler via the call stack window. In such a case, hardware tracing can come in handy.

We use the same application that we debugged in Ozone and enable instruction tracing via the parallel trace port.

You can do that in Ozone via **Tools | Trace Settings | Trace Source | Trace Pins**.

We let the application run and crash again. Vector catch is enabled, so we halt at the fault handler entry, and this time, we can see in the backtrace window the exact code path that has been taken.

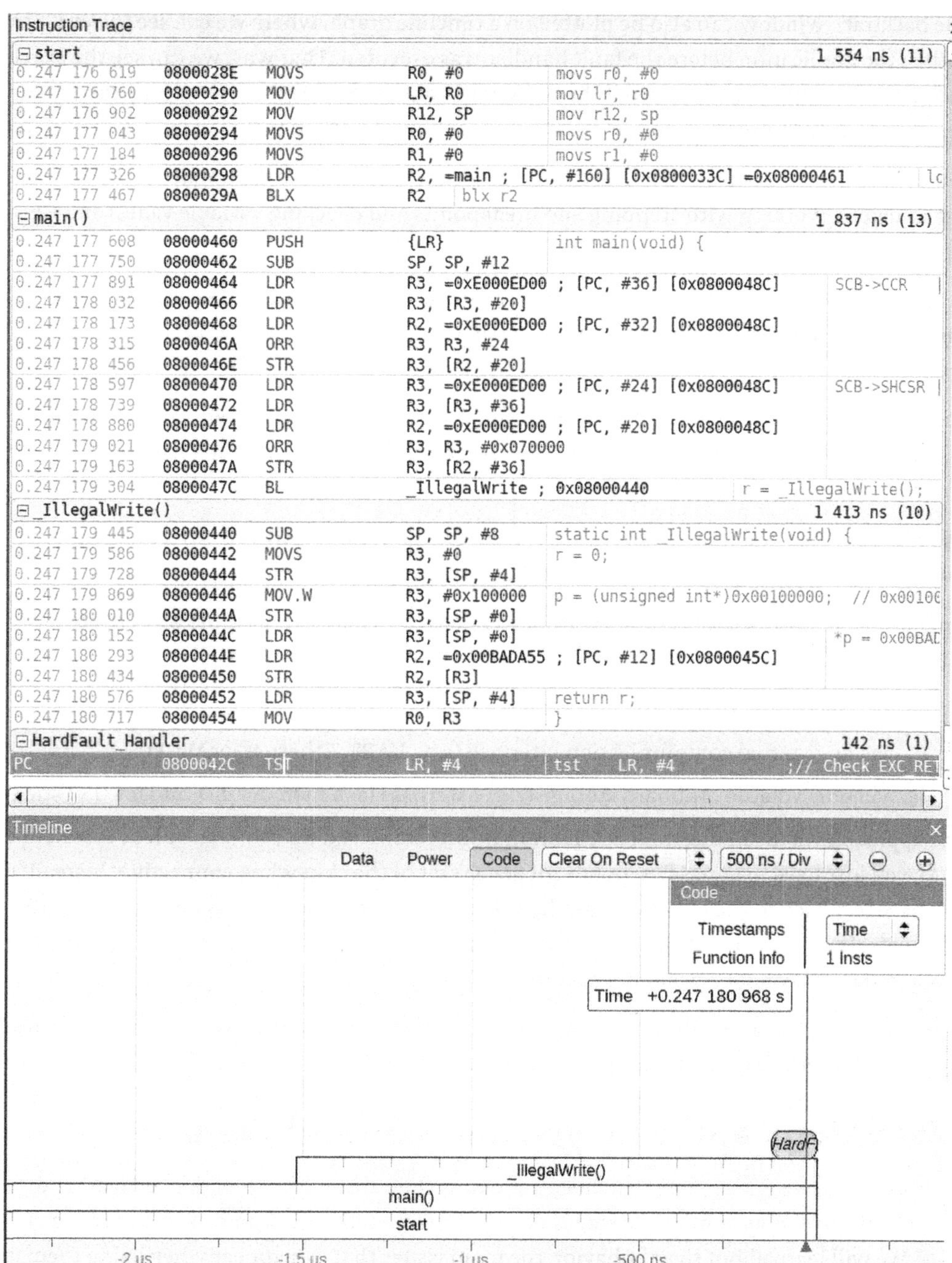

Figure 5.7: Ozone backtrace and timeline after crash

The backtrace window can also be plotted on a timeline graph, where we can see the exact call path of the application before the fault handler was executed. That way, we can see the exact code flow that our code took even if the call stack is not available. Also, we can get timestamps, depending on the target device, so we can even see how long each instruction took to execute.

Once we've got that information, we can again continue to analyze the application backward just as before, working with stepping and breakpoints and checking variable values and CPU registers to find out what has caused the crash.

So far, I have shown you what you can do with active debug access in a development environment. But what can be done about crashes if they appear in the wild when the product is released?

The most common answer is some flavor of logging. You would instrument your code with log calls at crucial system points and hope that after the chip crashes, you can retrieve the log and do a so-called post-mortem analysis.

Usually, a crashed system will stay in some recovery mode, so it will still be running in some way, but it will no longer execute the task that caused the failure.

You now need a way to extract the log from your system. There are multiple ways to achieve this. The most common ones are as follows:

- Via the debug interface
- Via an external communication interface (e.g., UART, Ethernet, or Wi-Fi)
- Via non-volatile on-board storage (e.g., external Flash memory, SD card, or USB stick)

The approach via the debug interface is straightforward. The data can even still be stored in RAM; you just have to make sure not to trigger a reset of the chip when connecting. Instead, you have to attach to the target device, then simply dump the memory region that stores the trace data. However, already shipped systems usually have their debug interfaces disabled, so this approach may not be available to you.

More common is to either dump the log to an SD card that can be removed for analysis or use an external interface that streams the log out constantly to some server.

Watchdogs and why you should feed them

In this section, we will explore watchdogs and how they are an often-overlooked feature on embedded systems as at multiple stages during development, they can kick in and ruin a good time. We will learn about their behavior, the main issues that can appear when using them in your application design, and how to detect them.

But let's start with the basics.

What is a watchdog?

A **watchdog** is a timer peripheral that is usually meant to recover a system after an unrecoverable failure by simply resetting the target device. It is mainly a safety feature and a last resort to recover target applications that have gone off the rails.

There can be on-chip watchdogs that are built in, as well as external off-chip watchdogs.

To configure a watchdog, you have to set a timer threshold after which a system reset will be triggered as a recovery measure. If you want to make sure that this only happens on real software failures, you must regularly update the watchdog. This is also called "feeding the watchdog."

While a watchdog is a very powerful tool, it also comes with certain caveats that must be considered.

The watchdog is first and foremost a timer that can configure a single timing trigger condition. You have to make sure that your whole application design takes into account that you have a timing ceiling that you may, under no circumstances, exceed under normal operation without feeding the watchdog. While this may sound straightforward, an embedded application may become more complex over time, and meeting the timing constraints at all times can quickly become challenging. So, whenever you decide to incorporate a watchdog into your design, make sure that you follow best practices so the watchdog does not become a cumbersome problem down the line.

Depending on your development approach, it might also be beneficial to disable watchdogs when debugging to avoid issues with it; otherwise, you might find yourself debugging "ghost" bugs that appear randomly due to the target being halted by the debugger. After finishing your debug session, you can then reenable the watchdog again. Additionally, if the watchdog is configured to trigger faster than your debug probe can attach to the target device, the system might not be debuggable anymore.

Another thing to consider is that on many target devices, the watchdog will be enabled by default after reset. So, you have to actively disable it in your system initialization if you don't want to use it; otherwise, it will be configured to some default timeout value, and you will run into unexpected system behavior.

Another pitfall is that some devices even offer multiple watchdog timers. So, even if you have made sure to disable or configure and feed one, make sure that there is not another one. The same is true for external watchdogs. Always double-check the schematics on the device's reset line and verify that the hardware department did not place a little surprise on the latest hardware revision.

Setup information

As an example setup, I will be using the Cortex-M Trace Reference Board and a J-Trace PRO V3 connected to it. You can find the example project that will be used here:

```
https://github.com/PacktPublishing/-Practical-Debugging-for-Embedded-ARM-
Systems/blob/main/Chapter5/Chapter5_Watchdog_Example_STM32F407.zip
```

The example project will enable a watchdog on startup but have no handlers that feed it. To see what is happening, we will use a second timer, SysTick, which will print a message every second with an increasing counter. The expected behavior is that the `printf` messages will appear at one-second intervals with increasing counter values. However, we will see how the watchdog will cause problems instead.

As debug software, Ozone V3.38g will be used. For software tracing, SystemView V3.62c will be used. As the IDE, I will be using Embedded Studio V8.26.

The software is running on a Linux Mint host system, but the software I am using is cross-platform compatible, so you can simply use what you are familiar with. How to set up each of these tools is described in detail in the software provider's documentation.

Analysis steps

Let's open the test application with Embedded Studio and run it.

We will see the following output in the debug terminal:

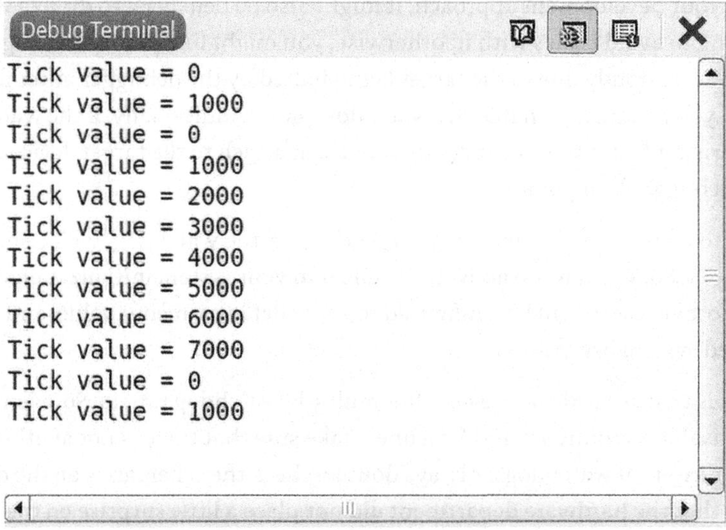

Figure 5.8: Debug terminal output on unfed watchdog

Additionally, *Video 5.1* is a recording of the running session.

To access the videos in this chapter, go to `https://packt.link/VHPD1`, or scan the following QR code:

Our expectation would be that the value increases indefinitely; however, it seems to reset regularly, which does not fit the example code, as this is the only function that manipulates the `_Tick` variable:

```
void SysTick_Handler(void) {
    _Ticks++;
}
```

The terminal output fortunately gives us the right hint of what is happening. But let's imagine that we do not already know the answer to this problem. What is this symptom showing us?

We see that a variable is being reset without our knowledge, and as far as we can tell from the source code, there is no other part of the code touching that variable that might cause this reset. A type issue can be ruled out, as the variable is an `int` and the printed values are too low to overflow the variable.

Of course, we could suspect the `printf` implementation, so we can debug it by setting a breakpoint on the `prinf` entry and trying out different input values, but we will quickly see that every value we try will be printed as expected. So, an error in the `printf` implementation can be ruled out.

Next, let's try to check who is accessing the variable at all. For that, we could use a data breakpoint that triggers whenever a change to the variable happens. We can see that there is only one location that will zero the variable, and it is the startup code where the zero `init` routine is initializing all static variables to zero.

This routine is only called after a reset. This is our first indication that something is going on with the device's reset.

Another way to make this visible would be to use data sampling, and we would see a clear periodic reset of the variable to zero.

Figure 5.9: Data sampling result of tick variable with unfed watchdog

To further verify this, we can set a hardware breakpoint at `Reset_Handler()` in the `STM32F4xx_Startup.s` file.

The expectation would be that we only end up here once after our initial reset and never again. But if we let the application run, to our surprise, we end up at that breakpoint regularly. With these various methods, we have made it clear now that something is resetting our device.

At this point, we have to check whether the reset is triggered internally or externally.

To check external reset sources, we have to resort to external measurement methods. For this, we can use an oscilloscope to measure the reset line of the target device. If it is triggered without being specifically activated by us explicitly, we have found the source of the problem, and all that is left is to check the schematics and see which external component might trigger the reset line. This can even happen accidentally, for example, when the transmission lines for high-frequency signals are not set up correctly or if we have external electromagnetic sources close to the reset line, such as electric motors, which can induce noise in digital signals and create issues.

But if there is no external reset trigger detectable, the problem is most likely an internal software reset that is being triggered.

At this point, our main suspect will be the watchdog timer, which can specifically trigger system resets.

If we check the reference manual of the STM32F407 that is used in this example, we will see that we have two watchdogs available: the so-called **Window Watchdog (WWDG)** and the **Independent Watchdog (IWDG)** [2].

We have to check both. For this, the peripheral register view in Embedded Studio can be used.

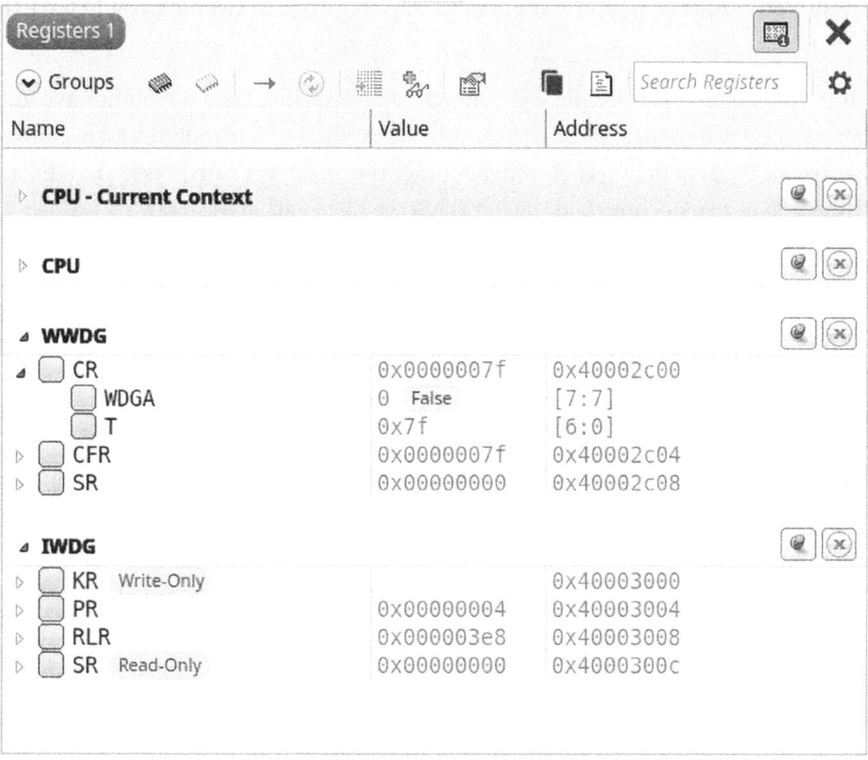

Figure 5.10: Watchdog register view

Checking the WWDG is straightforward. We just need to see whether the bit WDGA is set or not. As we can see, it is not set, and thus this watchdog is not enabled.

So, it is probably the IWDG. However, from the registers alone, it is difficult to determine whether the watchdog is active or not, as the control register is a write-only register and will not provide any information about the status of the watchdog. An indication can be that the PR and RLR registers vary from their default values after reset; however, you might also have a setup where you keep the default values, so this is not a guaranteed telltale.

That means that the only thing that we have left is to search within our code base to see whether the IWDG control register is ever being written to. Most IDEs have proper search functionality that can be used here.

In this example project, we will, of course, find the `Watchdog_Init()` function that way, where we will see that the IWDG is indeed being enabled.

As a sanity check, you can now comment in the `Feed_Watchdog()` function to verify the theory, and you will see that the application now behaves as expected and the watchdog is fed. Alternatively, you can, of course, comment out the watchdog `init`, which would have the same effect.

Now, bear in mind that this example scenario is device-specific, and you might have more luck with other devices' watchdogs, but this example nicely shows that sometimes, even though we have access to all kinds of debug tools and documentation, all we can do is make educated guesses based on our suspicions and the data that we have gathered so far.

If you are that deep into analyzing a specific bug, it is also a good time to start questioning everything about your setup and double-checking everything that is part of the setup. Sometimes, a wrong assumption may lead you down a completely wrong logical path, which will waste precious time.

> **Note**
>
> As an honorable mention, I want to recommend the so-called "rubber ducky debugging" if you are ever stuck during bug hunting [3]. It can work wonders sometimes.

RTOS multi-tasking pitfalls

In this section, we will look at RTOS task scheduling and how multi-tasking issues can be debugged.

Task priorities

Typically, an RTOS operates based on tasks. Each task has to be initialized, and during initialization, it gets a priority level assigned.

The priority level decides which task may be executed first if multiple tasks are pending at the same time. The higher-priority tasks execute first. If priorities are equal, the first task that is pending executes first. Let's assume that we designed an application where we have two tasks, where one should have a higher priority than the other. For simplicity, let's call them high-priority task and low-priority task. The expected behavior of such a system would be that the high-priority task always gets prioritized. If the low-priority task is running while the high-priority task is pending, the high-priority task can preempt the execution of the low-priority task.

If the priorities are accidentally flipped or equal, then the high-priority task can no longer preempt the low-priority task. In such a scenario, we may run into unexpected application behavior.

The same principle applies to internal and external interrupts on an MCU.

Such a bug is most commonly introduced when implementing new tasks or interrupts and not having a proper overview of all currently assigned priority levels.

Setup information

As an example setup, I will be using the Cortex-M Trace Reference Board and a J-Trace PRO V3 connected to it. You can find the example project that will be used here:

```
https://github.com/PacktPublishing/-Practical-Debugging-for-Embedded-ARM-
Systems/blob/main/Chapter5/Chapter5_Priority_Pitfalls_Example.zip
```

The example project will have the RTOS embOS running. It is based on the trace tutorial project that we were using in Chapter 4, but this time we tweak the task priorities to get the effect of inappropriate priority assignment.

As debug software, Ozone V3.38g will be used. For software tracing, SystemView V3.62c will be used. As the IDE, I will be using Embedded Studio V8.26.

The software is running on a Linux Mint host system, but the software I am using is cross-platform compatible, so you can simply use what you are familiar with. How to set up each of these tools is described in detail in the software provider's documentation.

Analysis steps

The example application usually has two tasks: one **high-priority task** (in the following screenshot, **HP Task**) and one **low-priority task** (in the following screenshot, **LP Task**).

If everything is set up correctly, the high-priority task should always be prioritized over the low-priority task, which we can see in the following SystemView recording:

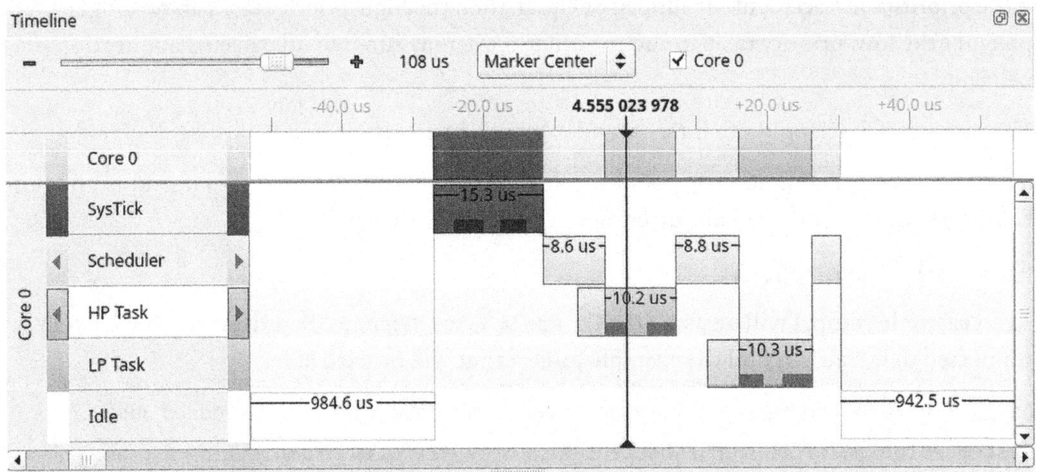

Figure 5.11: SystemView timeline of expected tasks switching order

As we can see, the SysTick interrupt triggers the RTOS scheduler, and the scheduler checks whether any tasks are pending. Both tasks are pending at this point, and due to their different priority levels, the high-priority task will be executed first.

But if we look at the example project, we will see that both tasks are actually set to the same priority, which obviously is a mistake if we are trying to have tasks with different priorities.

```
OS_TASK_CREATE(&TCBHP, "HP Task", 100, HPTask, StackHP);
OS_TASK_CREATE(&TCBLP, "LP Task", 100, LPTask, StackLP);
```

But how would this manifest in an application? In this example, two LEDs are blinking, one for each task, and with equal priority; sometimes, the high-priority task LED will switch slightly later than usual.

That does not sound too bad, but in a real-world application where, for example, the high-priority task should be reading out some time-critical sensor data and the low-priority task is simply a background logging task, it can become a big issue.

We might miss timing windows, get unexpected application behavior, experience increased system latency, and see overall system performance degradation, all because of a single task misconfiguration.

Now that we know what the symptoms are, how do we debug them?

First, we should try to find out what the expected behavior of our system is. Once that is established, we can check our interrupts and tasks and see whether we notice anything suspicious, such as locking mechanisms or potential long run times.

Next, it can be helpful to simply log whenever a task is scheduled; that way, we should already be able to determine which task might be the problematic one.

If we take it a step further, we can also try to log timestamps to get a feeling for task runtimes, and last but not least, we can check whether the RTOS offers any software tracing hooks that can be enabled. In the case of embOS, we have built-in SystemView code instrumentation, which we can make visible with the identically named analysis tool.

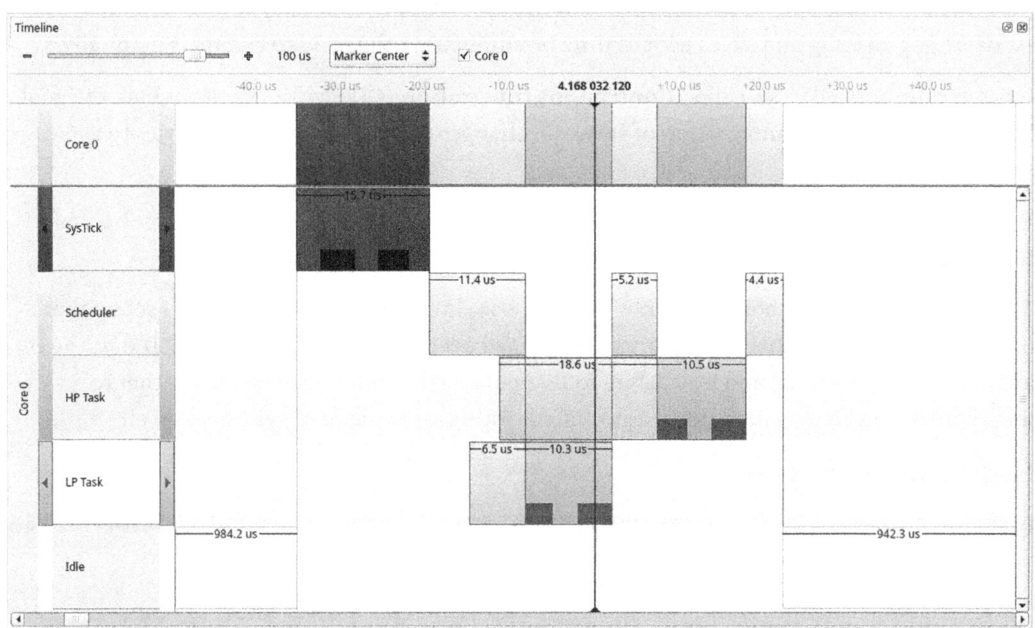

Figure 5.12: SystemView timeline showing priority issues

As we can see this time, the scheduler will first launch the low-priority task. During the execution of the low-priority task, the high-priority task will try to execute as well, but as its priority is not higher than the low-priority task, it must wait until the low-priority task is finished.

At this point, we should have sufficient information to pinpoint the issue with the task priority and fix it.

Debug tools and automated tests

In this section, we will go over automated testing and how debug tools fit into these setups.

What are automated tests?

Automated testing describes the process of using software tools or frameworks to execute predefined test cases for a software application automatically. It is a key resource in modern software engineering and saves a lot of time by eliminating the need to run tests manually.

It is typically applied in so-called **Continuous Integration** (**CI**) environments, where the goal is to frequently test the integration of software changes on shared code repositories to avoid problems.

While automated testing is widely used in software development on host PCs, it took a while for it to be adopted in embedded systems engineering on a broader scale.

This is not because the tooling was not there; it was simply more cumbersome to set up than on host PCs. However, this has fortunately changed over the last couple of years. Today, there are plenty of commercial and free debug tools available that offer one way or another to automate debug actions to perform automated testing on embedded systems as well.

Setup information

As an example setup, I will be using the Cortex-M Trace Reference Board and a J-Trace PRO V3 connected to it. There will be two example projects:

- The first example project will simply set up a timer peripheral and verify the initialization. However, in this section, the tests themselves are not the key points; how they can be automated and what information we can gather from the test outputs are. You can find it here: `https://github.com/PacktPublishing/-Practical-Debugging-for-Embedded-ARM-Systems/blob/main/Chapter5/Chapter5_STM32F407_UnitTest.zip`

- The second example project will be a trace tutorial project running embOS and launching two tasks. Two LEDs are blinking, one for each task. You can find it here: `https://github.com/PacktPublishing/-Practical-Debugging-for-Embedded-ARM-Systems/blob/main/Chapter5/Chapter5_J-Trace_PRO_CortexM_Tutorial.zip`

As debug software, Ozone V3.38g will be used.

The software is running on a Linux Mint host system, but the software I am using is cross-platform compatible, so you can simply use what you are familiar with. How to set up each of these tools is described in detail in the software provider's documentation.

Practical approach

In *Chapters 3* and *4*, we learned about all kinds of different debug features and ways to analyze an embedded system. But the typical use case is to use these features manually while debugging a system.

However, we will now learn how to use these features automatically for automated testing.

Let's first look at a typical CI pipeline and determine what its stages are to understand how automated testing fits in.

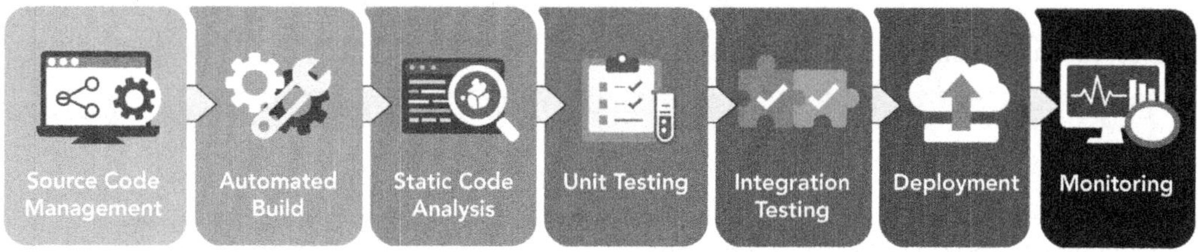

Figure 5.13: A typical CI pipeline

We can see that there are usually two test stages which, depending on the project's complexity, size, and how small a "unit" is defined, can also be the same step.

When reaching the test stage of a CI, you usually have your predefined set of tests that you want to run, and you want to run them automatically to save time and be able to react quickly to new bugs that have been added during development. This is important because the later a bug is caught in a development cycle, the more expensive it is to fix.

So, how can automated testing be achieved on embedded systems?

For this to be applicable, you need some way to automatically open a connection to your debug probe, control it to run tests automatically, and extract data.

Most debug probes will at least offer some sort of scripting interface, which typically offers several hook functions that can be used to force a certain behavior of the debug probe.

In some cases, there is even a **Software Development Kit (SDK)** available, which gives you access to the debug probe's functionality via an **Application Programming Interface (API)** that can then be used in your own tools to control the debug probe for something like automated tests.

Or, what is also very common is that the debug probes provide a GDB server, which can be used together with existing GDB clients that are widespread in different IDEs and debuggers.

In this section, I will focus on the scripting interface in Ozone, which uses the J-Link SDK API and allows us to easily create our own test scripts in Ozone without needing to implement all of the advanced debug features manually ourselves.

Unit testing with logging

The first example will initialize the TIM2 peripheral and verify its initialization.

TIM2 is a 32-bit general-purpose timer that can generate interrupt and DMA events under certain conditions. For more details, see the target device's reference manual [2].

Every key aspect of the test is logged via RTT. If you run the application manually and the test passes, the output should look like this:

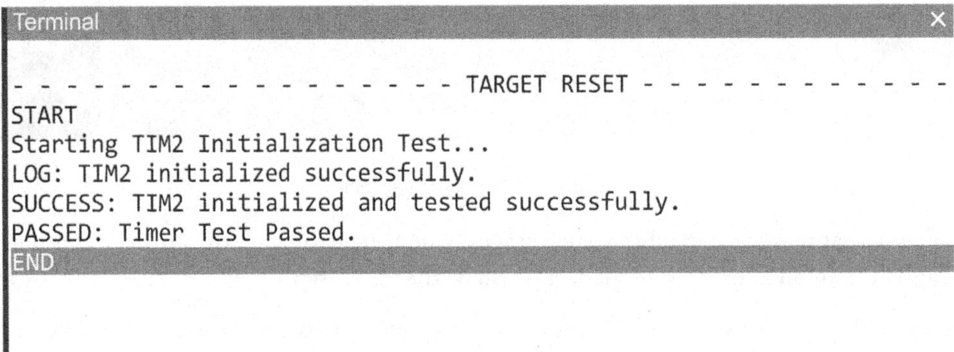

Figure 5.14: Ozone test log output

But how can this be automated? For this, we generate a new Ozone project with the Ozone project wizard. If we save the resulting project, we will receive a `.jdebug` file that is prefilled with various hook functions that can be used to change the default behavior of Ozone for certain debug scenarios.

The Ozone project is written in a C-like script language and allows you to replicate all actions that you could do with the GUI in this script.

So, let's now try to automate the example project with the goal of having it run automatically when Ozone is opened (e.g., via the command line), and the log output should be stored in a file.

To do this, we first have to make sure that the application runs automatically after the project is loaded.

For this, we add the following line to the `OnProjectLoad()` hook:

```
Debug.SetResetMode (RM_RESET_AND_RUN);
```

That way, we change the default reset behavior so that on debug start, the application will run uninterrupted.

Next, we want to define from where to where a test is running and perform an action on these triggers. For this, Ozone provides a trigger interface via breakpoints. For each breakpoint you set, you can define a custom hook function that will be set.

For simplicity, we set two breakpoints: one at the `main()` entry and one at the application exit.

For this, we add the following line to the `OnProjectLoad()` hook:

```
Break.SetOnSrc ("main.c:61");
Break.SetOnSrc ("SEGGER_THUMB_Startup.s:199");
//
// Set Function which should be executed once BP is hit
//
Break.SetCommand("main.c:61","OnBPHitMain");
Break.SetCommand("SEGGER_THUMB_Startup.s:199","OnBPHitExit");
```

This will set the aforementioned breakpoints and prime the triggers to execute the custom `OnBPHitMain()` and `OnBPHitExit()` hook functions, which looks as follows:

```
void OnBPHitMain(void) {
  Util.Log("---BP1 hit!---");
  Util.Log("---Starting test---");
  Window.Clear ("Terminal"); // Make sure test starts with cleaned terminal
  Util.Sleep(2000);
  //
  // Continue Application
  //
  Debug.Continue();
}

void OnBPHitExit(void) {
  Util.Log("---BP2 hit!---");
  Util.Log("---Exporting test data---");
  //
  // Export trace data
  //
  Util.Sleep(1000);
  Window.Show ("Terminal");
  Window.Export ("Terminal", "Testout.txt");
```

```
//
// Stop debug session and optionally close Ozone
//
Util.Sleep(5000);
Debug.Stop();
//File.Exit();
}
```

As final touches, we add some logging and sleeps to be able to track the test progress in the Ozone console. This is optional and mainly for demonstration purposes. In a real automated test scenario, this may be omitted, as you are only interested in the data output and the final test result, not some GUI logs.

For more information about the different commands, check out the Ozone reference manual [4].

If we now load the project either via the GUI or by opening Ozone via the command line and passing it the example Ozone project, the test will run through automatically and create a Testout.txt file in the project folder with the terminal log content.

> **Tip**
>
> Any GUI action you perform in Ozone will be logged to the Ozone console with its corresponding script command. So, if you are creating your own automation script, you can simply copy the commands from the Ozone console that you executed manually and place them in the correct hook functions in your project script.

The resulting .jdebug file can be found in the project folder as a reference.

Ok great, we now have learned how we can automate a project and extract our test report to a text file for further analysis.

As mentioned earlier, instead of using Ozone, you can also write your own test utility using the J-Link SDK or a GDB-based test framework.

Code coverage and profiling

In the previous section, we saw how we can do basic testing with logging, but what else can we do with additional advanced debugging features?

As we learned in *Chapter 4*, we also have access to hardware tracing on some target devices. By using instruction tracing in particular, and utilizing its code coverage and code profiling features, we can easily apply advanced automated testing to any integration test. In case of faults, we can quickly determine which part of the code is no longer working as expected.

For this, we can use the approach of the "golden sample." The main idea is that you record the expected output once and later compare all subsequent application changes to it.

That way, if your code changes have any impact on the overall code flow of the remaining application, this will be made directly visible, and you can inspect further whether this is expected or unexpected behavior.

In the case of expected behavior, you can update your golden sample once the changes are approved.

To use this approach in an automated fashion, we again must automate the debug session and export the trace data. We will use Ozone's automation capabilities as we did before, and the second example project from the setup section.

The second example project is simply the blinky trace example project that we used in previous chapters for demonstration. It is recommended to download the example files in this case to more easily follow along with the process.

The general approach is as follows:

1. First, we create a new Ozone project via the Ozone project wizard and save the project file. Then, we open it in a text editor.

2. This starts the same as in the previous example with the unit test logging. We change the reset default behavior of the debugger, add breakpoints, and add their corresponding custom hook functions.

3. The breakpoint locations are, of course, a bit different, as this is a different application, and the hook functions are exporting trace data instead.

The resulting file can be found in the example project folder under the name `Ozone_Automation.jdebug`.

We can export various types of information, including the backtrace information in CSV format, code coverage and profile reports in CSV format, and a more human-readable text output of the code coverage report.

The syntax from the example is as follows:

```
void OnBPHit2(void) {
  Util.Log("---BP2 hit!---");
  //
  // Export trace data
  //
  Util.Sleep(1000);
  Window.Show ("Instruction Trace");
  Trace.ExportCSV("./Instruction_Trace_Export.csv", 0);
  Profile.Export("./Profile_Trace_Export.txt", 0, "");
  Profile.ExportCSV("./Profile_Trace_Export_Funcs.csv", CSV_FUNCS, 0, "");
  Profile.ExportCSV("./Profile_Trace_Export_Lines.csv", CSV_LINES, 0, "");
  //
  // Stop debug session or close Ozone
  //
  Util.Sleep(5000);
  Debug.Stop();
  // File.Exit();
}
```

You can find the "golden sample" recordings for this project in the project folder under /
GoldenSamples. They are named Instruction_Trace_Export.csv,
Profile_Trace_Export.txt, Profile_Trace_Export_Funcs.csv, and
Profile_Trace_Export_Lines.csv, respectively. If you do not want to run the examples
yourself, you can inspect the example outputs to get an idea of their content.

To run the example project, hook up your J-Trace PRO to the Trace Reference Board and load
the project file in Ozone. The test will execute automatically. Once the test is done, you will
find the same four files in the project's root directory.

The next step is to compare the golden samples with your newly generated output files using a
so-called "diff tool". If you are on a Linux system, you can use the built-in diff tool. On other
operating systems, a popular variant is using the diff feature of Visual Studio Code.

If the tests ran as expected, the diff tool will verify that no change in code coverage data was
detected, and the new recordings match the golden samples exactly. Should there be
differences, the tool will highlight them so you can inspect them and analyze them further.

In our example test scenario, we started the project from the Ozone GUI. However, in a real-world setup, we would call Ozone via the command line, pass the automation project file as an argument, collect the output files, close the Ozone session, and diff the freshly generated test output with our golden sample files.

That way, we can get our test results in seconds, even when running on real hardware, which allows us to verify project progress in frequent steps. This gives us an edge over test environments that only do software testing due to the extra effort required and a lack of knowledge for performing automated hardware testing.

So, whenever available, I strongly recommend doing automated unit and integration testing on real hardware as well, to catch as many bugs as possible before it becomes too late and costly to fix.

Memory leaks, buffer overflows, and null pointers

This section will take a look at another classic set of bugs that often appear on embedded systems: memory leaks, buffer overflows, and null pointers.

We will learn what the typical causes of these bugs are and how they can be efficiently debugged with the introduced debug features.

While some of these bugs will trigger system crashes as discussed in the first section of this chapter, it may not always be best to analyze these bugs as shown there, so in my opinion, these specific bug types deserve to have their own section in this chapter.

When do these bugs appear?

Before being able to analyze the issue, we must first understand what these issues are and how they appear.

Memory leaks

Memory leaks will mostly appear when performing dynamic memory allocation in your target application.

So, anytime you allocate a memory section in your RAM, you have to actively manage that memory section. Once the allocated memory section is no longer used, you usually free it so the memory region can be reused.

But if you forget to free the memory and keep allocating more and more memory, you will at some point run out of available memory and encounter unwanted behavior.

One common scenario is that your memory usage is so high that further allocation by your application will fail, and thus parts of your application suddenly can no longer work as intended, and you might get parts of your application shut out.

This is further amplified by so-called memory fragmentation, where even if free memory blocks are available, you might not be able to allocate a certain memory chunk that is contiguous.

That is why many make the argument on embedded systems that dynamic memory allocation should be avoided if not necessary, as formulated in the **Motor Industry Software Reliability Association (MISRA)** C standard.

However, other programming languages, such as C++, require dynamic memory management for many of their standard library features, so it is often a trade-off between memory safety and convenience.

> **Note**
>
> As an honorable mention, I want to point out Rust, which is designed with a memory ownership model in mind to reduce these types of memory bugs entirely (if used correctly).

Buffer overflows

Another classic example is **buffer overflows**. As mentioned before, on bare-metal embedded systems, we are directly interacting with the hardware. So, anytime we use a programming language feature that interacts with system memory, we have to make sure that this memory segment is taken care of correctly throughout the entire application, or at least within the scope in which this memory segment may still be in use.

There are two types of buffer overflows:

- Stack-based overflows
- Heap-based overflows

These two types happen under similar circumstances. In both cases, we have a specific memory area available to us for usage, but the application tries to write outside of the available memory area, thus causing unwanted behavior.

The names of both overflow types give away what kind of memory locations are affected. Stack is used for things such as local variables and function control flow and does not require additional memory allocation. Heap, on the other hand, must be allocated and is usually used to store data structures that need to be valid for longer periods of time. In the case of buffer overflows, the symptoms of both types are very different, and thus the debug approach varies, as heap overflows may only cause issues during runtime without immediate indication of the issue, while stack-related overflows are usually more immediate.

> **Note**
>
> As an honorable mention, there are also arithmetic overflows, which can lead to over-
> or under-allocation of memory due to unexpected calculation results depending on the
> variable types. But let's keep it simple and look at statically allocated buffers in the later
> examples.

Null pointers

Null pointers are another bane of many applications, not only on embedded systems. However, as embedded systems often run in critical infrastructure, the consequences can be devastating.

A null pointer exception describes a fault scenario where the application tries to access an uninitialized pointer, which will have the value NULL, usually defined in embedded toolchains as a pointer to memory address 0x0. This can happen due to failed memory allocation, simply forgetting to initialize a pointer in a function, unhandled null pointer function returns, or dangling pointers in general.

Setup information

For the following examples, I will be using the Renesas EK-RA8M1 board with the on-board J-Link.

To build the applications, I will be using Embedded Studio V8.26, and for debugging, both Embedded Studio's debugger and Ozone V3.38g, depending on the information that I require from the system.

The example projects can be found here:

```
https://github.com/PacktPublishing/-Practical-Debugging-for-Embedded-ARM-
Systems/blob/main/Chapter5/Chapter5_RA8M1_Memory_Bugs.zip
```

This repository contains three fault scenarios that can be commented in to test different bug types.

The software is running on a Linux Mint host system, but the software I am using is cross-platform compatible, so you can simply use what you are familiar with. How to set up each of these tools is described in detail in the software provider's documentation.

Analysis steps

We will start with the `RunBufferOverflow()` buffer overflow test.

The example will show how a harmless-looking fill-up of an array can overflow and cause unexpected side effects. In this scenario, the array is stored in a struct, and the next member of the struct is a char array containing a string:

```
struct OverflowExample {
  int   aData[ARRAY_SIZE];        // Integer array to overflow
  char message[64];               // Adjacent string
};
```

Let's assume that this char array contains data that must not be changed by the application. Now, at some point, the application starts copying data into the aData array, for example, some sensor data. If the copy boundaries are not set up correctly, the copy will run out of bounds and start overwriting adjacent memory sections. In this case, it will alter the message that was stored in the message array.

We can see the issue in action in *Video 5.2*. To access the videos in this chapter, go to `https://packt.link/VHPD1`, or scan the following QR code:

Unfortunately, such a bug will not always be detected right away and may only cause issues much further down the line, far away from the actual faulty copy routine. In some cases, it might even trigger a hard fault, giving a clear sign that something is wrong. But there can also be cases where the application will not crash, but instead just start acting unexpectedly.

So, how do we approach such a bug?

First, we have to recognize that the application is not working as expected. As mentioned before, it is not always straightforward. What helps is to have a good understanding of the application that you are debugging, and ideally, you have utilized proven design patterns in your application to generally avoid such issues or at least make them visible if they appear.

One such approach is to have verbose system logging, so you can always check the log for anomalies. Another popular approach is so-called canary values. In that case, you place a specific value on the borders of buffers that serve no other purpose than buffer overflow detection. If that value is ever changed by the application, you know that a buffer overflow has appeared.

Once we have noticed that a buffer overflow has happened, we can try to narrow down the cause. If we have a scenario where a hard fault is triggered, it is a bit simpler, as we already know at least the code area where the unexpected value is accessed. That way, we can identify the buffer that is adjacent to the overwritten variable. You can either inspect the linker output file to see what buffer may have been placed close to the faulty data access or use the different variable and memory view windows in your debug software.

Next, we try to figure out which code part actually overwrites the memory in that section. For this, data breakpoints can be used and placed on the canary or symbol adjacent to the suspected buffer.

You can, of course, also do a dry analysis by using the search function of your IDE and see which code parts are working with the suspected buffer, but data breakpoints are way sleeker to use as they will point you directly to the cause of the issue. Additionally, data breakpoints will also be able to catch non buffer overflow related bugs like stray pointers accessing an incorrect address.

The last step of the analysis is to debug the code that is running before hitting the data breakpoint, for example, by stepping to see which write loop or `memcpy()` call is causing the overwrite.

In the specific example, we had verbose logging available, which showed us the symptom. Due to the simple nature of the example, we could quickly see that the `for` loop's exit condition loops one too many times. After adjusting the loop exit condition accordingly, the bug is fixed, and the application behaves as expected again.

> **Note**
>
> **Stack Limit Register**
>
> As an honorable mention, I want to point out that Armv8-M microcontrollers also have access to a **Stack Limit Register (SPLIM)**, which is a CPU register that can be configured to an address. This address is then the lowest legal address for the stack. If a stack action exceeds this address, we immediately get an exception. That way, we can at least quickly detect stack-based buffer overflows. So, if available, I recommend setting up that feature in your system initialization.
>
> Another software-based approach is the so-called **stack painting**, where the stack area is set to a distinct byte pattern. Then, after running the application, we can check the pattern and get a watermark value for the maximum stack usage during runtime until that point. That way, we can very easily measure the potential maximum stack usage of our application.

Next, we will look at the memory leak example. For that, we comment in `RunMemoryLeak()` and comment out `RunBufferOverflow()`.

The symptoms of memory leaks are usually that, at some point, an allocation will fail, or, if the memory management is not done cleanly, you might run into hard faults as illegal memory is accessed because no null pointer check was done.

We might also have certain system tasks fail to execute as expected due to a lack of available heap memory.

If we run the example with the active log, we will quickly see that only the first couple of allocations are successful and point to a valid address.

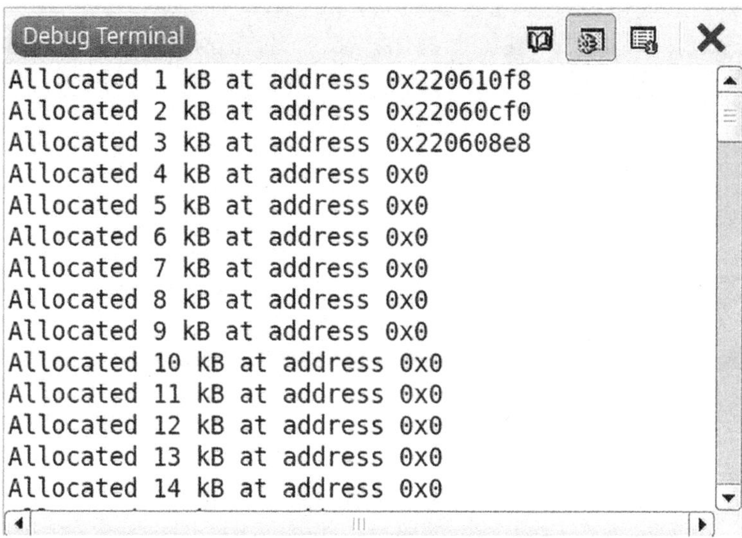

Figure 5.15: Log output of memory leak example

We see that 3 kB could be allocated, but the fourth and each later allocation are not successful. As I wrote the example, I know that the issue is that our available total heap memory is 4 kB and that we do not check the return value of the `malloc()` call to see whether the allocation was successful. But in a real-world application, this might happen anywhere.

So, to analyze and debug such issues, logging can be a very helpful tool.

There are also dedicated memory profiling tools that instrument the memory allocation and free actions.

SystemView is one such tool and can display any logged heap action in a practical window.

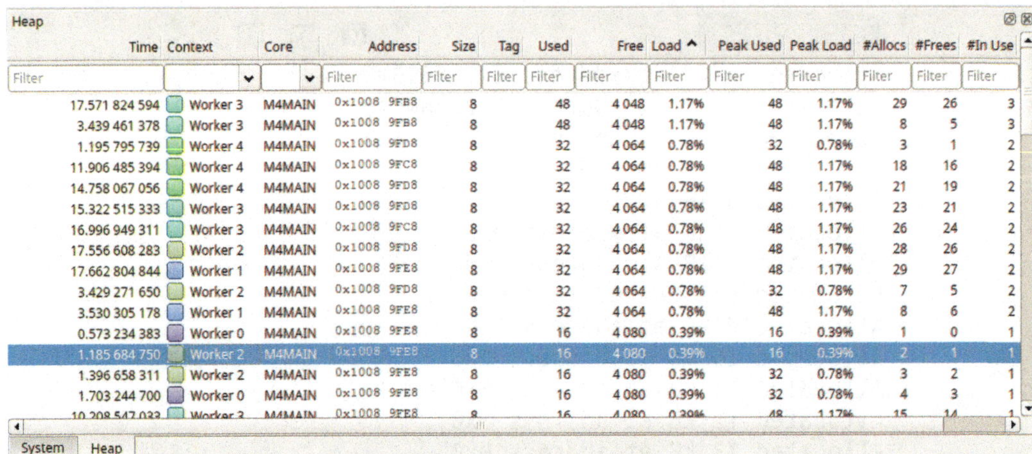

Figure 5.16: SystemView heap window

As we can see, we get a lot of additional information about memory usage on our running system: time, address, use number, number of allocations and frees, and many more. This can give great insight when trying to find memory leaks in your application.

Other methods include static code analysis, manual search for typical memory allocation functions, and debugging the code area around that memory allocation if it functions as expected.

Debugging memory issues is, unfortunately, not straightforward and requires a systematic approach rather than a fixed step-by-step instruction.

Next, let's look at null pointers.

As mentioned before, a null pointer exception can be caused by all kinds of oversights in an application.

To activate the example project, comment out `RunMemoryLeak()` and comment in `RunNullPtrTest()`.

Technically, we could do the null pointer test with `RunMemoryLeak()` by slightly altering the application and simply accessing the allocated memory in the memory leak without double-checking. In that case, we would also run into a null pointer exception once we run out of heap. But for simplicity's sake, I made another separate function.

If we run the example, we will run into a hard fault. At this point, we can apply all of the debug strategies we have already learned with crash analysis in general at the beginning of this chapter.

The main symptom of a null pointer will always be a resulting application crash.

Specifically with null pointers, though, it can be very helpful to have instruction tracing available to you, at least in buffer tracing form.

Typically, it would be sufficient to just check the application's call stack before the crash and work your way backward.

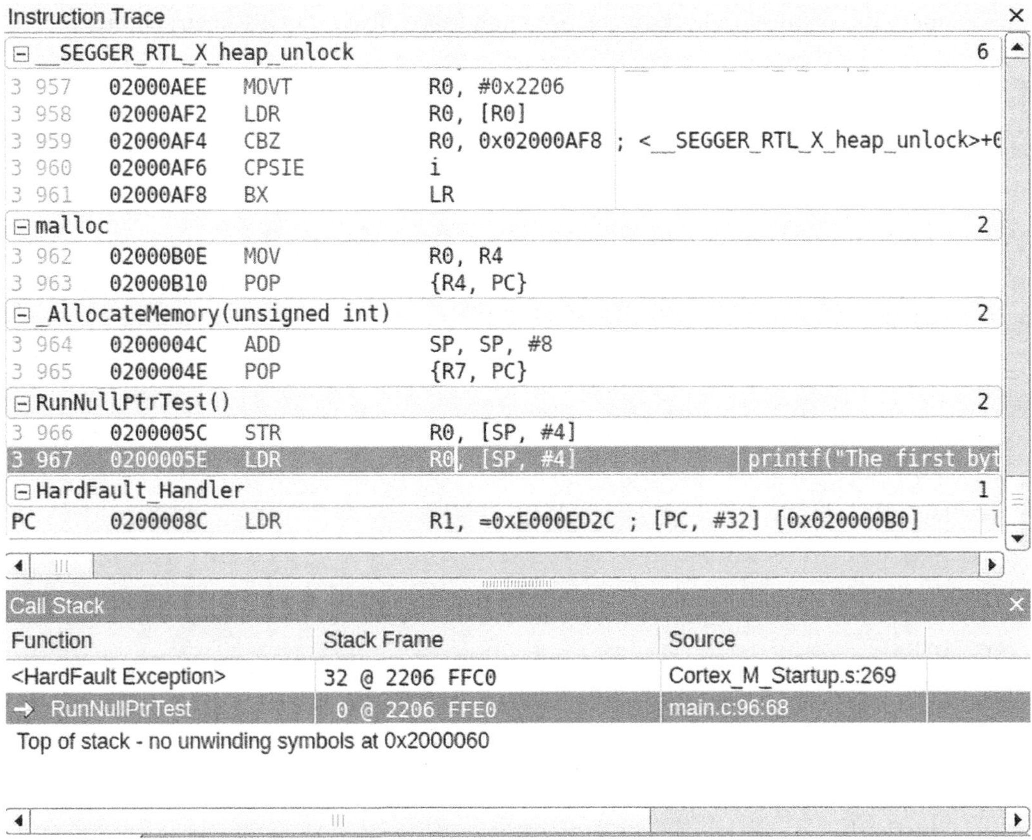

Figure 5.17: Ozone null pointer analysis

But as we can see, the call stack will only tell us roughly in which function the crash happened. With tracing enabled, we get additional insight into the application flow right before the crash, where we can see that a `malloc` was called, which in this case is directly the culprit for the null pointer access afterward, as we tried to allocate more memory than the chip has reserved for the heap.

All in all, memory bugs are unfortunately some of the most frequent bugs in embedded systems, because we're working directly with hardware using low-level languages like C and assembly. At the same time, these bugs are sometimes hard to track down, so it is crucial to utilize all tools available to you to extract as much evidence as possible for your specific scenario to find the cause of the bug quickly.

Another viable strategy is to use programming languages that provide some safeguards against such memory issues; specifically, Rust comes to mind, as well as C++ with smart pointers.

Communication errors

This section will focus on common communication interfaces as they are found in embedded systems and how they can be analyzed or even debugged.

What are common communication interfaces?

The most common interfaces (and protocols) that you can find on modern microcontrollers are the following:

- UART
- SPI
- I2C
- I3C
- CAN
- CAN FD
- USB
- LIN
- Ethernet
- Wi-Fi
- Bluetooth
- LoRa
- Zigbee
- Thread

At the top of the list, we find many classic wired interfaces that have been around for many decades. At the end of the list, we find more modern wireless interfaces that have mostly taken over the IoT space.

So, as we can see, the interfaces are plentiful, and potential bugs are just as likely.

General analysis approach

Looking at each interface individually and building example scenarios for each one would, unfortunately, exceed the scope of this book. Instead, I will try to offer general guidance on how to handle issues with the external interfaces of your microcontrollers and how to approach bug hunting.

Normally, with software-related bugs, the approach is straightforward and comparable to the other bug types that we have seen before. We first try to pinpoint the rough code area that triggers the unwanted behavior and then analyze it fully to understand the bug and thus provide a proper fix.

However, with external communication interfaces, we add external components to our system to which a debug probe suddenly has only limited visibility.

What I mean by that is that while we can still inspect the peripheral registers, work with breakpoints, and watch memory regions, we can't directly monitor the physical aspects of the interface, such as signal integrity or, in many cases, the protocol layer as well.

We simply rely on the peripheral that handles communication to do its job correctly.

But if it does run into issues, we are suddenly dealing with black-box aspects of the system that we plan on analyzing.

Luckily, there are external tools available that can give that extra insight into the communication signal and protocol layer, for example, oscilloscopes, logic analyzers, and other electrical measurement tools.

Some debug probes may even provide external trigger ports that can be connected to the trigger port of such an external measurement device, thus bringing the electrical world and the software debugging world closer together for more detailed inspection of problematic setups.

Now, let's summarize what we have learned so far in this final chapter.

We learned how to analyze system crashes, how to handle watchdogs, why priority management can be very tricky, how debug tools can be used for test automation, all about memory leaks and related issues, and, last but not least, guidance for analyzing communication interface errors.

Should you feel uncertain about specific debug techniques utilized in this chapter, make sure to revisit the previous chapters and check the references that you can find at the end of each chapter.

Some closing words

Congratulations, you made it to the end!

I hope you enjoyed the journey and that you learned at least one new thing with this book. Writing and sharing this information with a broader audience has been a very fulfilling experience, and I hope that at least some readers become better software engineers after learning about all of these different debug features and techniques.

In the end, we all use all kinds of engineering marvels in our daily lives, and the better equipped engineers are with tools and knowledge, the safer we are when using the products as end users.

My personal advice is that as an engineer, you should try to always stay curious, not be afraid to learn new things, and, if everything fails, don't forget to consult your rubber ducky for guidance.

With these closing paragraphs, until next time!

References

1. AN209: Using Cortex-M3/M4/M7 Fault Exceptions, AN209, Summer 2017: `https://documentation-service.arm.com/static/61084e4a3d73a34b640e31eb`

2. RM0090 Reference manual, STM32F405/415, STM32F407/417, STM32F427/437, and STM32F429/439 advanced Arm-based 32-bit MCUs, Revision 21

3. Rubber duck debugging: `https://en.wikipedia.org/wiki/Rubber_duck_debugging`

4. Ozone user manual (UM08025): `https://www.segger.com/downloads/jlink/UM08025`

Get this book's PDF version and more

Scan the QR code (or go to packtpub.com/unlock). Search for this book by name, confirm the edition, and then follow the steps on the page.

Note: Keep your invoice handy. Purchases made directly from Packt don't require an invoice.

6

Unlock Your Exclusive Benefits

Your copy of this book includes the following exclusive benefits:

DRM-Free PDF Version

Download DRM-free PDF and ePub copies of this book.

7-Day Packt Library Access

Get 7-day unlimited access to 8,000+ books and videos. No credit card required.

Available for first-time Packt+ trial users only.

Next-Gen Reader Access

Read this book on Packt Reader with progress sync, dark mode and note-taking.

Follow the guide below to unlock them. The process takes only a few minutes and needs to be completed once.

Unlock this Book's Free Benefits in 3 Easy Steps

Step 1

Keep your purchase invoice ready for *Step 3*. If you have a physical copy, scan it using your phone and save it as a PDF, JPG, or PNG.

For more help on finding your invoice, visit `https://www.packtpub.com/en-us/unlock?step=1`.

> **Note**
>
> **Note**: If you bought this book directly from Packt, no invoice is required. After *Step 2*, you can access your exclusive content right away.

Step 2

Scan the QR code or go to `packtpub.com/unlock`.

On the page that opens (similar to *Figure 6.1* on desktop), search for this book by name and select the correct edition.

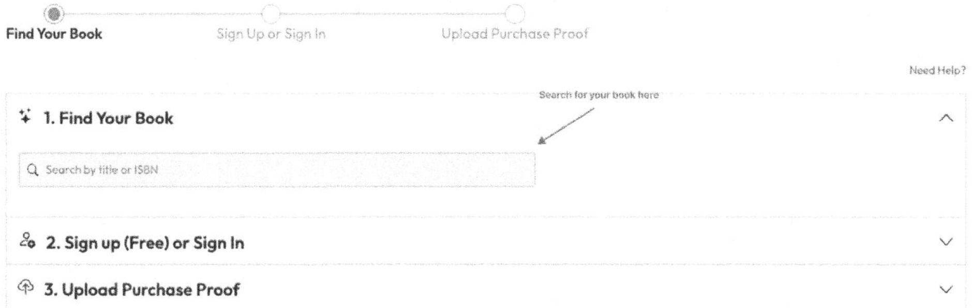

Figure 6.1: Packt unlock landing page on desktop

Step 3

After selecting your book, sign in to your Packt account or create one for free. Then upload your invoice (PDF, PNG, or JPG, up to 10 MB). Follow the on-screen instructions to finish the process.

Need Help

If you get stuck and need help, visit `https://www.packtpub.com/unlock-benefits/help` for a detailed FAQ on how to find your invoices and more. This QR code will take you to the help page.

> **Note**
>
> **Note:** If you are still facing issues, reach out to `customercare@packt.com`.

packtpub.com

Subscribe to our online digital library for full access to over 7,000 books and videos, as well as industry leading tools to help you plan your personal development and advance your career. For more information, please visit our website.

Why subscribe?

- Spend less time learning and more time coding with practical eBooks and Videos from over 4,000 industry professionals
- Improve your learning with Skill Plans built especially for you
- Get a free eBook or video every month
- Fully searchable for easy access to vital information
- Copy and paste, print, and bookmark content

At www.packtpub.com, you can also read a collection of free technical articles, sign up for a range of free newsletters, and receive exclusive discounts and offers on Packt books and eBooks.

Other Books You May Enjoy

If you enjoyed this book, you may be interested in these other books by Packt:

Reverse Engineering Armv8-A Systems

Austin Kim

ISBN: 9781835088920

- Understand the organization of Arm assembly instructions
- Disassemble assembly code without using C code
- Work with reverse engineering tools, such as GDB and binary utility
- Apply reversing techniques for both user space and kernel binaries
- Get to grips with static and dynamic binary analysis processes
- Get a solid understanding of the powerful debugging tool, uftrace
- Analyze TrustZone and the advanced security features provided by Armv8-A

The Insider's Guide to Arm Cortex-M Development

Zachary Lasiuk, Pareena Verma, Jason Andrews

ISBN: 9781803231112

- Familiarize yourself with heuristics to identify the right components for your Cortex-M project
- Boot code to efficiently start up a Cortex-M device
- Optimize algorithms with compilers, middleware, and other means
- Get to grips with machine learning frameworks and implementation techniques
- Understand security in the embedded space with solutions like TrustZone and TF-M
- Explore cloud-based development methodologies to increase efficiency
- Dive into continuous integration frameworks and best practices
- Identify future trends that could impact Cortex-M software development

Packt is searching for authors like you

If you're interested in becoming an author for Packt, please visit authors.packt.com and apply today. We have worked with thousands of developers and tech professionals, just like you, to help them share their insight with the global tech community. You can make a general application, apply for a specific hot topic that we are recruiting an author for, or submit your own idea.

Share your thoughts

Now that you've finished *Practical Debugging for Embedded ARM Systems*, we'd love to hear your thoughts! Scan the QR code below to go straight to the Amazon review page for this book and share your feedback or leave a review on the site that you purchased it from.

https://packt.link/r/1806673118

Your review is important to us and the tech community and will help us make sure we're delivering excellent quality content.

Index

Made in the USA
Monee, IL
07 July 2026